Jurisculture

Spyros Maniatis

Jurisculture
Greece and Rome

Gray L. Dorsey

Transaction Publishers
New Brunswick (U.S.A.) and Oxford (U.K.)

Library of Congress Catalog Number: 88-4752
ISBN 0-88738-237-1
Printed in the United States of America

Library of Congress Cataloging-in-Publication Data

Dorsey, Gray L.
  Jurisculture.

Bibliography: v. 1, p.
  Includes index.
  Contents: 1. Greece and Rome.
  1. Sociological   jurisprudence.   2. Law—History   and   criti-
cism. 3. Social change. I. Title.
K370.D67   1988   340'.115   88-4752
ISBN 0-88738-237-1 (v.1)

For Jeanne

Contents

Acknowledgments

My indebtedness to F. S. C. Northrop is beyond measure. I am indebted to him in general for opening my eyes to the issues of beliefs, meanings, and values that often underlie international disputes; for making it possible for me to begin the study of these issues under his supervision in the J. S. D. program at Yale Law School; for his unfailing support and confidence; for opening opportunities to me that I would not normally have enjoyed as a young law professor; for inspiration and friendship. I am indebted to him specifically, in this volume, for the mathematical approach to the pre-Socratics and Plato. I gratefully acknowledge the outstanding assistance of a doctor of the philosophy of science, Sandra Wawrytko. The responses of students over many years have helped me to clarify and refine the analysis herein.

Gray L. Dorsey

1

Origins of Jurisculture

Philosophy of law and social philosophy are products of European culture, even when it is assumed that they encompass the study of activities in other parts of the world. In the summer of 1976, the executive committee of the International Association for Philosophy of Law and Social Philosophy met in Paris to plan a World Congress on the theme Contemporary Conceptions of Law. A member of the committee proposed that subthemes should be Natural Law, Positivist Law and Marxist Law. The point was raised that the association is worldwide and perhaps members from Asia and Africa might feel that contemporary conceptions of law in their countries were being ignored. A western European member of the committee responded, with the audible approval of other members, that any activities in philosophy of law and social philosophy in Asia or Africa must necessarily fall within the three proposed subthemes. In the event, a fourth, catchall subtheme of Oriental Conceptions of Law was added to the program.

The desire to avoid such a built-in bias in comparing the organization and regulation of societies in Greece/Rome, China, and India had led the author to seek a structure of inquiry that would be, as nearly as possible, culturally neutral. The ultimate result was jurisculture. The first step was to look at the subject matter of philosophies of society and law, instead of looking at the ideas which compose such philosophies. What is a society? How is it organized and maintained? Is it a human creation or is it found among other forms of life? This line of thought led to an examination of current views of evolution.[1]

The general direction of evolution has been towards more complex organization and more effective exploitation of the life opportunities presented by the environments of the earth. Life on earth began some one to five thousand million years ago with one-cell organisms floating in a

1

warm, protein-rich saline solution. These organisms could take nourishment by chemical processes and could reproduce by cell division. By the time insects made their appearance, some two hundred million years ago, organization had become immensely more complex. Insects are characterized by a hard exoskeleton; a body divided into head, thorax, and abdomen; eyes, simple or compound; antennae; tracheae, or air tubes, opening from the exterior and branching among the tissues; and a highly developed central nervous system.

The insects are an extremely successful life form. They are able to feed, repel enemies, and reproduce in every imaginable habitat on earth, with the one exception of the ocean. Insects can live in the ground; in leaves, roots, and branches of plants; in fresh water; in tropical rain forests, arctic tundra, arid deserts, mountain slopes, and the seashore; and parasitically in animals and larger insects. Insects can walk, run, jump, fly, swim, and burrow. They can eat plants, animals, and dead organic matter, or they can live parasitically.

Of course the same insect can not live in all of these habitats. Obviously a grasshopper can not live inside a leaf; but creatures having the basic characteristics of insects do live inside leaves. Morphological modifications adapted creatures with insect characteristics to all the other habitats, providing wings for movement through the air to gather food or escape danger, and digging appendages for burrowing when the soil provided the only secure shelter. The insects, therefore, are not a single species, but a large class (about 450,000 species) within a phylum.

So far, we have talked of effectiveness in exploitation of life opportunities arising from increasingly complex organization and structural adaptation. These are changes in the organisms themselves. Society is the extension of organization beyond organisms to the relationships between organisms. In a society, sets of individuals perform activities that are auxiliary and complementary, each of the activities being performed by some of the members but benefitting all the members, thus increasing the effectiveness of the social group above the cumulative result attainable by independent individual efforts.

Among the social insects, sets of individuals are specialized to activities either structurally or behaviorally. Instances of structural specialization are the immense ovaries of queen honey bees, the gonads of drone honey bees who exist only to mate with the queen, the poison-equipped squirt-gun heads of soldier termites, the trail-marking pheremone glands of worker ants. Several instances of behavioral specialization are found at successive stages in the life of the worker honey bee. For the first three days of adulthood, they groom themselves, loiter, and are fed; from the third to the twelfth day they nurse the immature bees in the hive; from the twelfth to the eighteenth day they produce wax as needed for the comb; and from the nineteenth to the twenty-first day they guard the entrance to the hive. After the third week of adulthood, worker honey bees join the field force for the rest of their lives, and gather water, pollen and nectar.

The success of the insects in surviving and multiplying in nearly every habitat on earth is due to natural processes. By "natural" I mean processes that are independent of direction and control by the organisms involved. First came the evolutionary emergence of the characteristic structure of the insects—separate housings for the central nervous system, the respiratory system, and the digestive system, all protected by an external chitinous covering. Next came morphological adaptation (modifications of the structure) to the exigencies of different habitats, or environments. The basic structure proved capable of functioning effectively in a great many sizes, ranging from nearly microscopic up to about two inches in length (which approaches the limits of mass that a chitinous exoskeleton can contain), and with a great variety of modifications. Then came morphological and behavioral specialization of sets of individuals to specific, auxiliary and complementary activities. Morphological specialization develops the structure needed to perform an activity and suppresses structures not needed for that activity. Behavioral specialization reinforces a specific activity at a given time and inhibits other activities at that time.

Insect society is characterized by a high degree of necessity in the performance of socially beneficial activities and prevention of nonbeneficial activities. This necessity results from the specificity of qualification for each activity. Sets of individuals are naturally adapted and specialized to a specific activity throughout their lives or during a period in their lives. A set is so prepared for each of the auxiliary and complementary activities that, when simultaneously or serially performed, the result is a society. No sets of individuals are prepared for activities that would be harmful to the society, or that are not needed. The individuals do not participate in the direction and control of the activities. They have no part in determining their own qualification—what activity and how they shall be made capable of performing it. If an insect individual is to participate in society, indeed in life, it must do so by performing the specific activity at a given time for which it is qualified by processes beyond its understanding and control. Further, it would be meaningless to speak of an insect individual having the choice between performing and not performing the activity for which it is qualified, because natural control of reproduction provides an abundance of fungible individuals for any given activity, and when one drops out another takes over.

When the life form *Homo sapiens* appeared on the earth, just a few hundred thousand years ago, organization had again increased tremendously in actuality, but even more in potentiality. Adaptation was not fixed by natural processes. There are no human beings structurally adapted to specific foods or habitats; none with a ruminant's set of stomachs for grazing quickly in dangerous places and digesting slowly in safe places; none with lungs, mouth and stomachs suitable for living on plankton strained out of the sea as do the baleen whales, and none with winged, miniaturized bodies for catching insects in flight. There are no human subspecies of meat eaters, plant eaters, plankton eaters, or insect eaters. Similarly, specialization was not fixed by morphology and mechanized behavior. There are no human beings with natural weapons to slash, puncture, or poison enemies; no natural scouts, equipped with special glands to emit a trail-marking substance; no natural workers, equipped with pouches to carry food back to other members of the social unit, or compelled by stimuli beyond their control to sweep the city streets for the first three days of each full moon during the twenty-first through the twenty-fifth years of their lives. Even with respect to reproduction, structural specialization is not specific to the point of excluding other activities, and performance is not dominantly controlled by natural stimuli which are timed to produce breeding and births in naturally determined seasons.

In *Homo sapiens* structure was generalized, the brain was greatly enlarged, and adaptation and specialization became dependent upon cultural processes. Human beings learned to accumulate information, to verify or disprove it, and to transmit it in space and time. We learned about the various environments and alternative responses to problems of existence in each; how to make various responses, and how to teach others to do so; how to make and use sophisticated tools; how to distribute auxiliary and complementary functions by voluntary assumption or compulsory assignment; how to organize and direct cooperative projects; how to regulate and govern interpersonal relationships.

In short, we human beings are not directed to ends, and to means for achieving those ends, by natural processes beyond our own direction and control. Given general, cumulative intelligence and great plasticity of behavior, human beings, to a high degree, have taken over from nature the direction and control of events external to our own organisms. This area of external responsibility includes searching out life opportunities, identifying them as ends to be sought, and devising means to achieve them. The means are both material and nonmaterial. The material means is technology. The nonmaterial means is society. For example, when it was discovered that copper and tin heated together produced tools and weapons that were far superior to shaped stones or annealed copper, the artifacts and processes for making bronze became the technology of the day. But, in order to exploit the opportunities opened up by the discovery of bronze, human beings had to form and preserve societies in which the auxiliary and complementary activities would be performed that would obtain and protect sources of copper and tin, make bronze, and effectively utilize the resulting tools and weapons. Functions to be performed included hunting for new sources of tin and copper, digging and carrying from the mines, making bronze, protecting mines, smelters, and persons and possessions, gathering and preparing food, building shelters.

The first inference arising from the conclusion that human societies are organized and regulated by cultural, instead of natural, processes is that human beings live in the world as they understand it to be, not as it is independent of human awareness. The second inference is that societies are formed to serve perceived needs, not to enable members to live in accordance with truth. The first inference has long been accepted as fact. The second challenges a deeply held view most forcefully expressed by Plato in the *Republic,* namely, that only those who know pure truth are qualified to govern. Natural law philosophy, which embodies this view, has been the central tradition of western civilization.

It follows from these two inferences that ideas which are adapted and used in organizing and regulating society must meet two criteria: they must hold promise of facilitating satisfaction of perceived needs, and they must be consistent with the current understanding of reality. Ideas which meet these two criteria and which pervasively seep into the consciousness of a people become basic beliefs in that they constitute the reality that must be reckoned with, like it or not. The seeming necessity of basic beliefs helps to replace in human societies the necessity of performance that characterizes societies directed and controlled by the natural processes of structural adaptation and structural and behavioral specialization.

The generalized structure, high and cumulative intelligence, and plasticity of behavior of human beings carries potentialities of more complex, flexible, effective organization of society, but they also carry potentialities for obstructive and destructive actions, nonperformance of assigned actions, and simultaneous conflicting actions. In early societies the absence of actual necessity was overcome by the seeming necessity of taboo, custom, totemism, and naturalistic religions.

The period from 600 to 300 B.C. encompasses three simultaneous, but radically different, seminal surges of systematic thought about the reality in which we live. In Western civilization, this was the period of the Greek presocratic philosophers and Plato and Aristotle. In India, the period spans the creation of Buddhism, the reinvigoration of Jainism, and the formation of the six great systems of Hinduism (Nyaya, Vaisheskika, Sankya, Yoga, Purva Mimamsa, Vedanta). The same period in China covers the lives and work of the founders of Confucianism (Confucius and

Mencius) and Taoism (Hsun Tzu, Lao Tzu and Chuang Tzu). A study, over many years, of the organization and regulation of societies in these three civilizations has convinced me that there are five fundamental beliefs which have significant effect upon social and legal systems: the nature of the world, human nature, what is most worth having, how to know, and who can know.

Jurisculture is a method of reasoning and a field of study. As a method of reasoning it synthesizes philosophy and empirical investigation. Neither sets of meanings derived without reference to observed events, nor sets derived solely from observation, are considered to be a sufficient basis for understanding and anticipating human events. Jurisculture looks to sets of meanings derived by adaptation and use of fundamental beliefs to organize and govern human cooperation. Beliefs considered to be fundamental are those about the world we live in, what is most worth having, human nature, how we know, and who can know. The subject matter of jurisculture is not sets of ideas about just and effective societies and legal systems; it is historical attempts to form and govern authentic, effective, and just societies.

The cultural means by which human beings form and regulate societies include cognition of reality, identification of life opportunities, selection of a dominant opportunity, and organization of institutions, processes, and procedures to ensure that goal-directed actions will be performed and conflicting or destructive actions will be deterred. A society is authentic when the cluster of goals of the dominant life opportunity and the goal-directed actions are consistent with a shared view of reality. A society is effective when the goal-directed actions facilitate achievement of the goals of the dominant life opportunity. A society is just when goal-directed actions and decisions are governed by principles that acceptably serve and reconcile claims and demands of individuals and groups and that can be credibly derived by accepted canons of reasoning from prevailing fundamental beliefs.

Note

1. Julian Huxley, *Evolution, The Modern Synthesis* (New York and London: Harper & Brothers, 1943); Pierre Teilhard de Chardin, *The Phenomenon of Man* (New York: Harper & Row, 1965); Jacques Monod, *Chance and Necessity,* trans. A. Wainhouse (New York: Knopf, 1971).

2

Early Beliefs and Social Structure

The first challenge to human beings to go beyond accumulated common sense experience—such as tool-making skills and hunting tactics—may have been awareness of animation and order. Animals are born, grow, are strong and able, reproduce, decline, and die. Plants spring from seeds, flourish, flower, produce fruit, go to seed, wither, and die. The sun, moon, tide, seasons have their cycles.

The Indo-European people that migrated into the Greek peninsula and the Aegean islands from 2,000 to 1,000 B.C. ascribed the animation and order of the perceived world to an anthropomorphic source. Certain resourceful, powerful, and practically wise men were thought to possess the animating and ordering power in some measure. Perhaps such a man could control a boat in a raging storm, direct the course of a battle, or bend others to his will. When such a man died, it was believed, his soul lived on as companion and protector of his descendants. He became the founder of a family, the Greek eponymous hero. Not only did the genius of the original house father remain near his grave to assist, guard, and guide those who supplicated it, but also his active power was passed through the blood to the oldest son, thus residing in the successive paterfamiliases in perpetuity.

What some men possessed in some measure, personalized gods of nature were believed to possess in full measure. The power to cause grain to germinate and fructify was personalized as the god of grain. Personalized gods were believed to control all events which in later Western civilization were believed to be subject to natural causes and effects. The gods of physical nature were originally the creation of each family and were as local and exclusive as the domestic ancestral gods. Later the sharing of an Apollo or Demeter which had given notoriously beneficial service to a great family facilitated the amalgamation of families into gens, tribes, and then city-states.[1]

7

These beliefs about the world and human nature were prevalent at a time when the dominant life opportunity was to settle down from a seminomadic existence to fixed agriculture. More secure and comfortable shelters could be built. The family's entire store of possessions and supplies need not be carried about. Life could be less precarious, more bountiful. As the Indo-European Greeks, or Hellenes, drove out the earlier residents in the peninsula and islands, they came into control of suitable land. What more was needed in order to form an effective farming society?

It is reasonable to assume that the Hellenes could borrow from others. Surely they had the opportunity to observe farming by the people they dominated and replaced. This borrowing would include tools and techniques; how to make and repair tools; how to work the soil; and how to gather, store, and process crops. Perhaps the borrowing included the modes of organizing and directing the various tasks involved in agricultural production, processing, and marketing. We know, for instance, that in the course of the diffusion of industrialization, latecomers borrowed from the British commercial and economic institutions as well as machine designs.[2]

We can assume that the Hellenes were observant and prudent, that they accumulated and made use of practical experience. Early Greeks and Romans used natural plants and extracts to ward off insects and rodents and to protect against fungal diseases, such as blight and mildew. Democritus recommended that seeds be soaked in leek juice before planting. Smoke from burning chaff or dung, extracts of lupin flowers or wild cucumber, and amurca (the residue remaining after the oil is drained from crushed olives) were used as pesticides. Plants that reputedly repelled airborne or earth-dwelling predators, such as bay, cedar, cumin, fig, garlic, ivy, and pomegranate, were juxtaposed to row crops and vines.[3]

Given that the Hellenes wanted the benefits of fixed agriculture, controlled suitable land, could learn skills and techniques by observing others, and were capable of accumulating practical experience, they needed to distribute sets of individuals to the auxiliary and complementary activities required for successful agriculture. In nonhuman societies this distribution is done by natural processes; in human societies it is done by cultural processes.

The designation of persons to make decisions important to the survival and well being of the whole group is crucial to the organization of society. The sets of individuals entrusted with such responsibility must be those deemed capable of making decisions that will be generally beneficial, not just personally advantageous. Those who have this capability will be the ones who have a correct understanding of the reality which shapes life opportunities and dangers and who know what is most worth having.

For the early Hellenes, the significant reality was the external, material world—the world of wind, rain, sunlight, grain, domestic animals, human beings, birth, death, growth, decay, work, war. It was the world of common sense experience, in which a table supports dishes, a misplaced stool barks shins, a plow turns soil, a sickle cuts grain, a spear pierces flesh. What was most worth having in such a world was beneficial control over physical events and human events. Since it was believed that gods caused events, knowledge of how best to get along in such a world was limited to those who could efficaciously approach the gods—to learn what they intended to do or to persuade them to act in advantageous ways. The natural inference from the belief that some men possessed in some measure the animating and ordering power of the gods was that these men could most efficaciously approach the gods. Therefore, the eponymous heros and successive eldest sons, who inherited the power of the founding father, were entrusted with all important decisions.

This distribution of competence to make important decisions determined the structure of society in early Greece and Rome for a thousand years. Younger sons, unmarried daughters, wives, clients, and slaves had access to the gods only through the paterfamilias of the family into which they were born or to which they were attached. All ordering was from the gods and was mediated through a paterfamilias who tended the living spirit of his ancestor in the hearth fire ever burning in the center of the family dwelling, supplicating the gods and consulting them through the auspices. It was not that religion was all important per se, but that the practice of religion was the only way to get a handle on the world. Accordingly, all important decisions were placed on the paterfamilias. He was the lawgiver and judge, the economic manager and the war leader by virtue of being the head of the family religion. Unemancipated sons, unmarried daughters, wives, and slaves were subject to the authority of the paterfamilias. Free men who, for any reason, had been cut off from the family into which they were born attached themselves to a paterfamilias as client. The paterfamilias's authority was full, and could be abused; but a person who was not a member of a family had no one to intercede for him with the gods and was, therefore, a creature without identity, protection, or rightful place.

The assignment of important decisions to paterfamiliases and the grouping of all others under their authority served to divide the total social group into sets of workers, each under the direction and control of an authentic leader. But this did not organize society in a way that was particularly apt for fixed agriculture. Placing all important decisions on a number of dominant males is equally appropriate for nomadic life. What was needed, additionally, was a principle that would distribute these sets of persons across the face of the available farm land so that no plot would be untilled and none would be claimed by more than one set of workers.

The territorial distribution of the family-organized sets of workers was accomplished by adaptation and use of a belief in the locality of gods. The dead ancestors, who were worshipped in their own right and were viewed as links to the gods of nature, were buried near the house, establishing a perpetual bond between a family and a particular piece of land. The fields surrounded the house and a strip of unplowed ground surrounded the fields. In this outer strip boundary stones were set into holes that had been prepared with the ashes of sacrificial fires, marking the limits of the jurisdiction of that family's gods and ancestral spirits. The adjoining field was the domain of the gods and spirits of another family.

The bond thus established by the gods between a family and a plot of land could not be broken by human beings, even by the paterfamilias who possessed the active personality of the demigod founding father. The land belonged to the family. Family did not mean just the living persons clustered under the authority of the paterfamilias, but included the continuity of generations of housefathers in perpetuity. Land, the principal source of wealth, was the "property" of the continuity-of-generations family, claimed and marked off by the gods of that family and preserved to its members for their sustenance and well-being forever. The current paterfamilias did not "own" the property, and the succession of generations did not involve inheritance of property. The current paterfamilias could not sell the family land, or alienate it by will; and the succeeding paterfamilias could not refuse an estate that was a net liability. What was passed on was not the property, but the active personality of the preceding housefathers, which qualified the incumbent to approach the gods who controlled events. Daughters, being unable to receive the active personality of the housefather, were excluded from all decision making, including management of the family land.

This patriarchal organization of society prevailed wherever the belief in local anthropomorphic gods prevailed. The pre-Hellenic peoples in the Greek peninsula had a matriarchal culture in which name, relationship, and status depended upon the mother, and daughters possessed the right of inheritance.[4] The laws of many Greek city-states retained traces of this older culture.[5] The patriarchal principles were more completely and pervasively implemented in early Roman law.[6]

Gods of nature, like the household gods, were local, although their domain did not long remain restricted to the fields of a single family. Agnatically related families and physically adjacent groups of families found it possible to adopt an Apollo, Demeter, or Athene that had acquired prestige because of the success of the family it served, as the god of a city-state which replicated the structure of the family. But the god that caused rain to fall on Athens was never viewed as the same god that caused rain to fall on Sparta. The city-state was the largest social unit the Greeks were able to form, and the locality of the gods was the principal limiting factor.

The Greek concept of the locality of the gods may have been formulated precisely in response to the need for a directing and justifying basis for distributing specific sets of persons to particular pieces of arable land. We do not find this locality in the gods of the Indo-European people who conquered the Indian subcontinent. They came from the same geographic region and shared with the future Hellenes a belief in gods that controlled events and were susceptible to human supplication expressed through worship before the sacred fire. But in India the efforts to bring the efficacy of the gods down to earth for human benefit was not limited to seeking, at family altars, the intervention of gods with local efficacy. The efficacy of the gods reached throughout India, but was more intense at the sites of Hindu temples and at certain sacred places of pilgrimage. In the temple the domestic altar was not uniquely associated with any group or locality, but represented the suppliants of the whole earth, and the fire from the terrestrial altar was merged with the fire from the celestial altar, supplicating gods of boundless jurisdiction to bring their efficacy to bear upon the problems of the worshippers. Perhaps most significant is the fact that the human activity for which divine efficacy was invoked in the Hindu temple did not need to be distributed spatially and fixed to specific plots. The help of the Vedic gods was sought not in aid of cultivation of the earth, but in aid of achieving "moksa"—liberation from the cycle of reincarnation. The regime of worship and meditation in pursuit of liberation did not require the exclusive appropriation of plots of land as did fixed agriculture. Hundreds of thousands could worship in the same Hindu temple in the course of a year and millions could bathe in the Ganges.[7]

Regardless of why the concept of the locality of the gods was originally formulated, there can be no question of its tremendous impact upon social structure. The source of the capacity to make wise decisions, and therefore the source of authority in all human activities—economic, social, legal, and military—for more than a thousand years throughout the Greek and Italian peninsulas and the islands of the middle and eastern Mediterranean remained the gods who had the power to control events and who served communities no wider than the city-state. Ortega y Gasset points out that Cicero said that all of the great achievements of the Roman republic throughout its history were secondary in importance to the initial establishment of "those two excellent foundations of our commonwealth, the auspices and the senate."[8] The auspices were the means by which the will of the gods was sought, and the senate was composed of the heads of family religions, who in the city-state as at the family altar had the right to consult the gods.

So long as the belief in local anthropomorphic gods constituted the reality in which people lived, it was inconceivable that governing authority should be placed in anyone but magistrates drawn from the heads of patriarchal families. In Rome the right of the people to be free from abuse of governing power was early implemented by creation of a tribune of the people, who could veto the act of any magistrate. But the paralyzing effect that modern experience would lead us to expect from such a veto power did not occur. For over three and a half centuries the tribunes exercised their power responsibly because they shared the general belief that only patricians could exercise the positive, directing role because only they could approach the gods.[9] When this belief lost its thrall the republic, in which the senate ruled, came to an end and the Roman emperors, without warrant of authority rooted in generally held belief, ruled with the compulsions and attractions of force, wealth, deception, gratitude, and hate subsequently annotated by Machiavelli.[10] The Greek city-states, unable to overcome the locality of divine warrant to govern, could not organize a panhellenic society and polity that could organize and regulate activities to exploit the opportunities of Mediterranean-wide trade and commerce. The resulting Peloponnesian wars mortally weakened the Greek city-states.

Notes

1. Numa Denis Fustel de Coulanges, *The Ancient City*, trans. Willard Small (Garden City, N.Y.: Doubleday & Co., 1956), pp. 120–126; Carl W. Westrup, *Introduction to Early Roman Law* (London: Oxford, 1944), 1: 35–38; A. H. J. Greenidge, *A Handbook of Greek Constitutional History* (London: Macmillan & Co., 1896), Ch. II; Kathleen Freeman, *Greek City States* (New York, N.Y.: W. W. Norton & Co., 1950), pp. 17–18.
2. Knut Borchardt, "The Industrial Revolution in Germany, 1700–1914," trans. Hammersley, in *The Fontana Economic History of Europe*, ed. Carlo M. Cipolla (London: Collins, 1973), 76 at 82.
3. Allen E. Smith and Diane M. Secoy, "Forerunners of Pesticides in Classical Greece and Rome," *Journal of Agricultural Food Chemistry*, Nov.-Dec., 1975, pp. 1050–1055.
4. Johann J. Bachofen, *Myth, Religion, and Mother Right*, trans. Ralph Manheim (Princeton, N.J.: Princeton Univ. Press, 1967),pp. 75, 235.
5. Hans J. Wolff, "Greek Law," in *Encyclopedia Britannica*, 15th ed. (Chicago: Encyclopedia Britannica, Inc., 1975) 8: 398, 400; Hans J. Wolff, "Greek Legal History—Its Functions and Potentialities," 1975 Wash. Univ. Law Quarterly, pp. 395, 404–407.
6. Bachofen, pp. 117–118, 235, 237; Wolff, "Greek Law," p. 400; A. R. W. Harrison, *The Laws of Athens: The Family and Property* (Oxford: Clarendon Press, 1968), p. 70.
7. Stella Kramrisch, *The Hindu Temple* (Calcutta: University of Calcutta, 1946), pp. 3–7, 21–28.

8. Jose Ortega y Gasset, *Concord and Liberty,* trans. Helen Weyl (New York, N.Y.: W. W. Norton, 1946), p. 21. The reference is to Cicero's *The Republic*, 2. 10.
9. Ibid., pp. 42–46.
10. Mikhail I. Rostovtsev, *Rome,* trans. J. D. Duff (New York, N.Y.: Oxford, 1960), pp. 226–247, 266–290.

3

The Presocratics

What is real?

The presocratic Greek philosophers sought a definitive answer to the question, What is real? This question appears to start with a blank slate, assuming nothing; but the presocratics were conditioned and limited by the culture and the society in which they lived. They did not make a systematic investigation of the external material world, the world of the spirit, the world of comprehensive harmony, and other worlds that have figured in the cultural history of the earth, and then conclude that one of these was real and the others illusory. The aphorism of the first of the Greek natural philosophers, Thales of Miletus, that "All things are full of gods," symbolizes the rejection of the view that events are caused by anthropomorphic gods who are outside things, pushing them about.[1] But to reject anthropomorphic gods as the answer to the question of what causes the animation and order in the perceived world was to accept the implicit assumption that the most important knowledge to pursue was what makes things tick in the common sense world of experience. In short, the presocratics *assumed* that the external material world was the significant reality.

Thus did it occur that the foundations of Western civilization were laid by natural philosophers, instead of spiritual philosophers as in Indian civilization, or philosophers of comprehensive harmony as in Chinese civilization. It was not that the external material world was the sole and exclusive focus of attention. The early Pythagoreans believed in the transmigration of souls. But the bits and pieces of thought that were considered most significant over time—that were preserved, passed on, replied to, disproved, verified, accumulated, and built upon—were those that sought to explain the nature of the external, material world. Bertrand Russell points out that the atomic theory of Democritus of Abdera, who flourished

14

about 420 B.C., was the culmination of an answer, one hundred and fifty years in the making, to the question first addressed by Thales, namely, How can we account for the changing world around us?[2]

There is no redundancy in assuming that the external material world is the significant reality and pursuing the question, What is real? The assumption refers to a prevailing belief, which began as an idea but had so pervasively seeped into the consciousness of a people that it constituted reality itself—the world they lived in.[3] The presocratics sought to understand that world so that they could live as satisfactorily as possible. Pursuit of the question, What is real? by the presocratics was the first step in the long process that eventually resulted in the view that physical events are the result of physical causes, that these causes and effects are rationally ordered, and that human beings are rational creatures and therefore capable of knowing what effects will follow from what causes.

Presocratic pursuit of the question, What is real? began the process of replacing an understanding of the nature of the external material world based on belief in the anthropomorphic gods with an understanding based upon systematic investigation, which entailed development of established canons of logic and rhetoric. The systematic investigation sought to learn what was irreducible and ultimate and caused everything else in the external material world to be as it is. Systematic investigation in Western civilization, which in the modern period grew into the science that has given human beings such tremendous power over the biosphere and the geosphere,[4] makes new discoveries by following a few themes, which function as presuppositions suggesting previously unobserved facts that can then be searched out and verified. Among these themes are simplicity, continuity, symmetry, order, change, constancy, limit, purpose.[5]

The presocratics made use of these themes. They began with the external material world known by the senses. The simplest explanation of gross sensible objects would be that bits of some primary sensible object combined in various ways to compose all other things in the world. Obvious candidates for the primal stuff, out of which all else was formed, were earth, air, fire, and water. These are the four significantly different aspects of the sensible world, and processes of what appeared to be transformation of one into another could be observed. Water becomes solid when cold and evaporates when heated. Fire consumes solid substances and currents of hot air rise from the burning fuel. Air can be observed to contain greater and lesser amounts of moisture and conjecture could easily suggest that it condenses into water and then into solid substances, which often were observed to be saturated. The reverse of this process would suggest that earth was the primary substance.

In the sixth century B.C., various philosophers proposed one or another of these observed substances as the primal stuff, beginning with Thales, who chose water. In general, philosophers in the city-states of the Ionian coast took the position that the real is stuff, that is, that it is material. In addition to the suggestions that one or another of the four common sense substances was the primal stuff, there was a proposal that the primal stuff did not resemble any kind of observed matter, but was something more fundamental,[6] and proposals that more than one of the observed substances were primary. (Empedocles suggested that earth, air, fire, and water were primary, together with two agents that divided them or bound them together, which he called strife and love. Anaxagoras suggested that there was a mixture of earth, air, fire, and water in everything.)[7] The view that the external material world is composed of one or more sensible material objects is identified as Ionian, although not all the philosophers who held this view were from Ionian city-states. The view is also customarily called materialist, although earth and air, hot and cold, and love and strife were lumped together because distinctions had not yet been made between matter, principle, and quality.

Within fifty years after Thales initiated the Ionian view that all things are composed of bits of material objects, Pythagoras established a brotherhood of philosophers who took the position that form, not matter, is primary. Particularly persuasive was Pythagoras's discovery that proportions in the length of a lyre string bring the order of harmony out of the full range of sound. The octave is obtained by halving the length of a string, which is expressed by the arithmetical ratio of 2:1. The ratio of the fifth is 3:2, the fourth 4:3. These consonances are still fundamental in Western music. This discovery suggested that the significant differences in things are not caused by matter, which is common to all, but by quantitative proportions. Harmonia in the body, or health, was formulated as the correct proportion between opposite qualities such as hot and cold, wet and dry, bitter and sweet.[8] Similarly, the composition of the physical world was not accomplished solely by matter. Like sound which has not yet been limited by quantitative proportion, matter not limited by quantitative proportion is chaotic.

Pythagoreans conceived of chaotic unlimited matter not as part of the sensible physical world but as existing in a surrounding void. The primal stuff of the world came into existence when some of this potential or inchoate matter was given form by being quantitatively limited. When the unlimited first met with or was acted upon by limit (in a way not explained by the Pythagoreans) and thus became a material unit with magnitude, it began to "breathe in" the inchoate matter in the surrounding void, and limit successively formed the second, third, fourth, etc., units. The Pythagoreans expressed numbers by arrangements of dots or pebbles, like the patterns found on dice or dominoes, or like the patterns formed by the ten pins in the game of bowling, or the fifteen balls in pocket billiards. Bertrand Russell points out that the "Latin world 'calculation' means 'a handling of pebbles.' ''[9] If one arranges lines of pebbles each having one more than the preceding, beginning with one, the result is a triangle. Thus, the shape of a series of both odd and even numbers is a triangle.

FIGURE 3.1

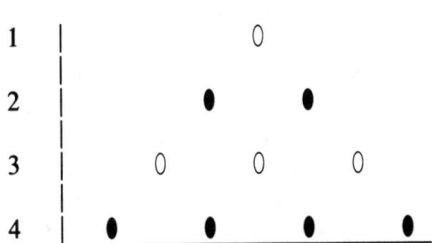

The shape of successive odd numbers, such as 1, 3, 5, 7, etc., is a square;

FIGURE 3.2

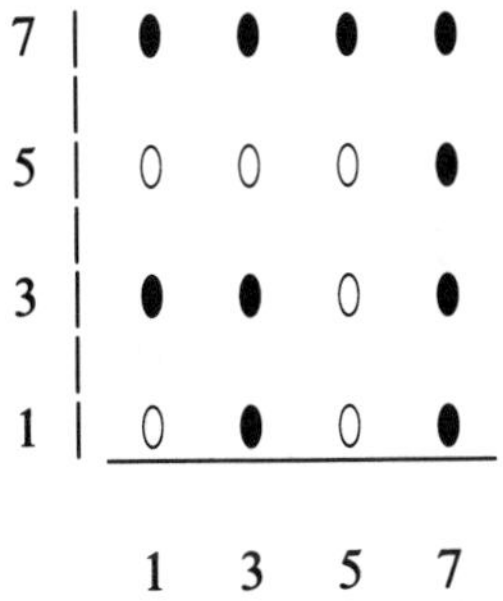

```
7 |  ●  ●  ●  ●

5 |  0  0  0  ●

3 |  ●  ●  0  ●

1 |  0  ●  0  ●
   _____

      1  3  5  7
```

and the shape of successive even numbers is a rectangle.

FIGURE 3.3

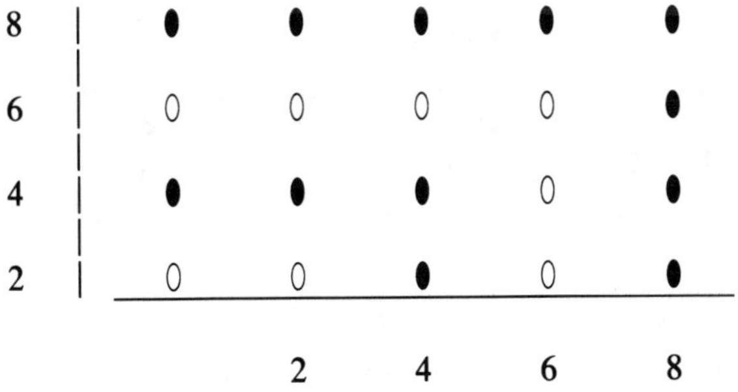

```
8 |   ●    ●    ●    ●    ●

6 |   0    0    0    0    ●

4 |   ●    ●    ●    0    ●

2 |   0    0    ●    0    ●
   _____

       2    4    6    8
```

Given the fact that the Pythagoreans used this kind of notation of numbers, and the fact that distinctions had not yet been made between matter, principle, and quality, it is not surprising that they believed that the first unit generated not only the number series, but also the physical universe, points becoming lines, then plane surfaces, then solid bodies.[10] It was this understanding of number as form and limit that the Pythagoreans meant when they said that the real is number. For the early Pythagoreans, this meant that the external material world was explained in terms of some irreducible ultimate sensible object. Perhaps it would be more accurate to say that, for the early Pythagoreans, number meant not form, but formed matter, because Aristotle tells us that the Pythagoreans supposed numbers to refer not to abstract units but to sensible substances having spatial extension or magnitude.[11] The view that the external material world is composed of bits of formed matter, designated by number, is identified as Italian, because Pythagoras, forced to leave his native Samos during the reign of the tyrant Polycrates, established his society at Croton and then Metapontion, both at the foot of the Italian peninsula. These Pythagorean societies flourished during the last third of the sixth century B.C.

At the turn of the sixth and fifth centuries B.C. Heraclitus added to the Ionian view of primal matter and the Italian view of primal material number, a view that utilized the themes of motion, change, and stability. The few fragments remaining of Heraclitus's writing are enigmatic apothegms, and it has always been a subject of speculation whether he ever set out his position in a systematic treatise. It would have been difficult because he was calling attention to an aspect of physical reality that could not be precisely identified and discussed without the use of concepts which had not yet been formulated. Examples of the fragments, preserved in the writings of Stobaeus, Plutarch, Plato, and Aristotle are:

Disease makes health pleasant and good, hunger satiety, weariness rest.

And as the same thing there exists in us living and dead and the waking and the sleeping and young and old; for these things having changed round are those, and those having changed round are these.

Things taken together are whole and not whole, something which is being brought together and brought apart, which is in tune and out of tune; out of all things there comes a unity, and out of a unity all things.

It is necessary to know that war is common and right is strife and that all things happen by strife and necessity.

And some say not that some existing things are moving, and not others, but that all things are in motion all the time, but that this escapes our perception. (Said by Aristotle, referring to Heraclitus.)

Therefore, it is necessary to follow the common; but although the Logos is common the many live as though they had a private understanding.[12]

Heraclitus began with the Ionian idea that earth, air, fire, and water are transformed into each other. He generalized this insight with respect to all pairs of opposites, up and down, wet and dry, hot and cold, health and disease, hunger and satiety, weariness and rest, young and old, living and dead, sleeping and waking, and then he sought to explain the mechanism or principle that operated in this continual flux and produced sufficient order and stability to make it meaningful to speak of health or water or up or cold.

Heraclitus moved the cumulative presocratic investigation of nature towards the abstract by putting forward a problem that could not be answered by supposing the existence of primal sensible bits of matter or material number. Heraclitus's answer was not very satisfactory, but tremendously powerful insight was required just to state the problem. The Ionian theory of the transformation of substance was the beginning of an atomic theory that was not developed until modern times. To say that earth, air, fire, and water are elementary substances and that they are transformed into each other and combine to form all other substances appears, at first blush, to be hopelessly primitive. But it is not that far from the mark.

Water, a chemical compound of hydrogen and oxygen, is constituent of the cells of all animal and vegetable tissues and of the crystals of many minerals. Air is a mixture of gases. Of the ten nonvariable components of air, oxygen constitutes 20.9 percent by volume. (Nitrogen constitutes 78.1 percent, and the other eight collectively constitute one percent.) Of the eight variable components of air, water constitutes up to 7 percent. (Carbon dioxide constitutes up to one percent and the other six collectively constitute less than one percent.) The first few miles of the earth's crust is estimated to consist, to the extent of 99 percent, of ten chemical elements. Of these, oxygen constitutes 46.6 percent. Oxygen by volume makes up over 90 percent of the rocks and minerals, mainly as oxides of silicon and aluminum. (Silicon, at 27.6 percent, and aluminum, at 8.1 percent, are, next to oxygen, the most abundant chemical elements in the earth's crust.)[13]

The ancient notion that fire is an element persisted through the middle ages until Francis Bacon in his *Novum Organum,* published in 1620, said that the notion was false. In 1660 Robert Boyle demonstrated experimentally that burning cannot occur in the absence of air, but it was not until 1783 that Lavoisier stated the modern theory that burning is a process in which oxygen enters into chemical combination with the substance undergoing combustion. Heraclitus, nearly 2,300 years before Lavoisier, had the intuition that fire was not a substance, but the process that kept all things moving back and forth between opposites.[14]

Modern chemical theory solved the problem of motion, change, and stability by the combination of chemical elements into compounds and the combination of these into cells and crystals. Until the breakthroughs of nuclear physics in this century it was assumed that atoms of the chemical elements were ultimate, irreducible, and unchanging. We now know that atoms are not the basic building blocks of physical nature and the search continues for subatomic unchanging particles. Nevertheless, the nuclear and electromagnetic forces that hold the components of an atom together are strong and therefore atoms of the chemical elements, for most purposes, can be treated as eternal. An atom of oxygen may have reposed for eons in some iron oxide, been released by a refining process, spent some time in the air, joined two hydrogen atoms to form a molecule of water, descended as a rain drop into sedimentary soil, entered into the cells of vegetable tissues until it came to reside in Plato's liver, been liberated when his body decomposed, shuttled back and forth between air and cell tissues for another twenty-four centuries, until it came to its present location in the muscle tissue of the third finger of my left hand with which I produce s's, w's, and x's as I type these words. If I try to imagine comparable journeys of each of the billions of atoms in my body during their eternal existence, I understand what Heraclitus meant by the constant flux of things.

Atoms of all the elements in molecules and cells of an animal are held in a structured relationship to each other within an identifiable entity for a sufficient length of time so that there is no problem about use of language in speaking of a gross entity as an object, such as a "cat", or a "mouse", or a "person", rather than having to refer to billions of atoms of oxygen, hydrogen, or iron, for example, in transit, as it were.

Heraclitus's question was this: What stabilizes the motion of all things, the change of everything into its opposite, the continuing flux throughout the universe, so that anything has a sufficiently fixed existence that it is meaningful to speak of it as an object, with a name that refers to something that is, instead of things that are constantly coming to be? The modern answer to this question is that the stability of biological "things" is caused by the forces of strong and weak interactions that hold the nuclei of atoms together and control radioactive decay; by the electromagnetic force that holds atoms, molecules and liquids together; by the integuments, ligaments, skeletons, and muscles that hold cells and multicell animals together, plus the processes that sustain life and therefore nourish and replenish these biological substances. In short, biological entities are the result of stabilizing forces, substances, structures, and processes of the biosphere. Similarly, geological entities are the result of stabilizing forces, substances, structures, and processes of the geosphere. Additionally, the force of gravity prevents objects from floating off into space.

Coming at the beginning of the 2,500 years of Western civilization's investigation of the physical world, Heraclitus could not have an inkling of any such answer. The modern answer began with the Newtonian distinction between a real world, with absolute, true, mathematical time, space, motion, and matter, and an apparent world with relative, apparent, common time, space, motion, and matter. When the real world and the apparent world are distinguished, the perceived light and heat of the fire are understood to be caused by the motion of atoms in the real world. The distinction between the real world, known indirectly, and the apparent world, known by the senses, was made in a preliminary form by the presocratics, but not until after Heraclitus's time. Therefore, Heraclitus could not solve the problem of stability in the midst of motion and change by means of unchanging substances, either in the sensible world or in a real world.

Plato solved the problem raised by Heraclitus, or rather he gave up on solving it. He could not anticipate the solution of modern chemistry and physics because, although he distinguished between the sensible world and the real world, he believed that the real world contained nothing of substance, no material objects moving in time and space, but only pure forms, or ideas. His real world contained only "intelligibles." That which had materiality according to Plato was in the sensible world and only approximated the real forms, or ideas, of the intelligible world. Therefore, Plato held that everything in the sensible world was constantly coming to be—it never attained the stability within the flux of motion and change so that it could appropriately be referred to as an object. But if it was not a material object, what was it? In order to answer this question Plato invented the distinction between substance and quality. He used "quality" for the first time in the *Theaetetus,* 182a, and he said that what appear to be material objects in the sensible world, such as the Ionian elements of earth, air, fire, and water, are in fact sets of qualities, by which he meant wetness, dryness, heat, cold, etc.[15]

After this rather long explanation of the modern answer, and brief reference to Plato's view that the question could not be answered, Heraclitus's answer is anticlimactic. He held that the tension—the "war" or "strife"—between opposites causes the stability that makes it meaningful to speak of objects instead of components constantly in flux. The answer was not taken up as a lasting part of the cumulative investigation of the physical world in Western civilization. But Heraclitus has been remembered for the intellectual power that enabled him to pose the question.

Characteristics of the Real

Some time between 490 and 475 B.C., about one hundred years after Thales inaugurated Western philosophy, Parmenides wrote a poem with a philosophical message that had profound effect upon Western civilization, not by causing the emerging view of reality to be something it would not otherwise have been, but by illuminating its essential characteristics. The message of Parmenides' poem was: What is, is. The part of the poem called "The Way of Truth" consists of a logical deduction of the meaning of being. However, the title of the poem, "On Nature," indicates that Parmenides was discussing being incident to his pursuit of the irreducible or ultimate in the reality of the external material world. It was quite common for presocratic philosophers to title their disquisitions on the irreducible or ultimate essence of reality, "On Nature."[16]

The Characteristic of Noncontradiction

Parmenides was originally a Pythagorean but he saw a logical inconsistency in explaining the existence of primal stuff by reference to a void. Matter exists; the ultimate and irreducible primal stuff of which it is composed must also exist—must have being. That which does not exist is not-being. If stuff is, if it exists, it must be everywhere. If stuff is everywhere there is not any place where stuff is not, and therefore, no place where anything that is not stuff can exist. Void, which is not stuff, must therefore not exist. Being excludes its opposite, not-being. "I would hold thee back," says Parmenides, "from that way also on which mortals wander knowing nothing, two-headed; for helplessness guides the wandering thought in their breasts; they are carried along, deaf and blind at once, altogether dazed—hordes devoid of judgement, who are persuaded that to be and to be-not are the same."[17]

How pervasive and fundamental is the dependence of creatures of Western civilization upon the exclusion of logical opposites! Lucien Levy-Bruhl said that the law of contradiction is the hallmark of modern logical thought. The primitive person lived in a world in which nothing was impossible or absurd but, on the other hand, no two things were connected in a way that could be verified or predicted. Such a world could not be known; it could only be experienced. For this reason, Levy-Bruhl said the law of participation characterizes the primitive world, whereas the law of contradiction characterizes the modern world.[18]

One need not accept Levy-Bruhl's typology to acknowledge that the knowable certainties of an external, real world require the law of contradiction. We could not train the young to distinguish between reality and illusion if we did not constantly make them accept the limits and implications of the law of contradiction—that the same thing cannot at the same time be both here and there, wet and dry, cold and hot, etc. And the same fact cannot simultaneously be true and false. Every legal system of the world which takes its heritage from Western civilization contains a rule that forbids taking the benefit of both affirming and denying the same fact.[19]

The Characteristic of Being[20]

From common observation, gross objects come into existence and pass out of existence. If, as repeatedly suggested, there is a primal stuff, it had to be explained how primal stuff could be the cause of gross objects. One possibility was that differences in gross objects are caused by changes in primal stuff. This position was indicated by Heraclitus's statement that all things are in a constant state of flux—that even primal stuff was not fixed, constant, but changed over time. Plato tells us that all the presocratics, prior to Parmenides, took this position.[21] Parmenides rejected change in primal stuff, saying, "Nor will the force of true belief allow that, beside what is, there could also arise anything from what is not."[22] Therefore, he reasoned that there can be no coming-to-be and no ceasing-to-be. What *is* exists not only now, but also of necessity always has existed and always will exist. Being excludes becoming.

The powerful predictive capability of modern science depends upon the existence in the material world of a *necessary,* not just an occasional or incidental, connection between a cause and an effect. For example, in a Newtonian frame of reference the state of a system (such as the solar system) at a certain time (T_1) can be uniquely and completely described by a statement of positions, masses, and velocities of its entities, and then, using Newton's laws of motion, the state of the system at any given time in the future (T_2) can accurately be predicted.[23] This kind of accurate prediction would not be possible if the entities in the system changed their mass, or if a given mass changed the magnitude of its gravitational pull between T_1 and T_2. To say that entities are characterized by being is to state that such changes cannot occur. The assumption has been experimentally verified hundreds of thousands of times.

The assumption of being, therefore, states something true about the nature of the material world. This truth is necessary to a rigorous and precise understanding of the material world. When the epistemology of the

Newtonian world, in the hands of Locke, Berkeley, and Hume, reached the conclusion that the human mind could not know persisting entities in an external material world, Kant invented the "forms of sensibility" and "categories of the understanding" which he placed in the knowing mind in order to provide a plausible rationale for the experimentally verified fact that mathematical physics gives human beings a real grip on a real world.[24]

That the modern physical sciences have not been playing with shadows and illusions is shown by the tremendous power that modern science and technology have developed over the geosphere and the biosphere. The recent developments in the physical sciences have qualified, but not eliminated, the characteristic of being as a fundamental assumption about the material world. Einstein's discoveries taught us that Newton's laws of motion hold only for special cases, not throughout the universe. Quantum mechanics taught us that microcosmic systems have to be described statistically. Nuclear physics taught us that the nucleus of the atom is not the ultimate, irreducible bit of matter. But it is still assumed that there are irreducible building blocks that have fixed characteristics, in terms of which the whole of the physical universe can be correctly known and beneficially controlled, although it is getting more difficult, at the subatomic level, to distinguish between matter and energy. The importance to the postindustrial state, which seeks to utilize available power over the geosphere, of the discovery of the ultimate building blocks of the world, is shown by the fact that in the United States the search is carried out by teams of the most highly qualified scientists, supported by government grants, working on apparatus supplied by the government at a cost of millions of dollars, and the discovery, or even the rumor of a discovery, of a new subatomic particle (or characteristics) is front-page news.[25]

The Characteristic of Universality

In Parmenides we see the transition from cosmogony to cosmology, but also we see the working out of a single generally accepted cosmology. The shift from a cosmogony to a cosmology involves the development of conceptions and of logical analysis adequate to enable a people to move from unverified beliefs to systematic knowledge as the basis of understanding the physical world. A cosmogony is a generally accepted, unexamined and unexaminable belief about the origin of the world. It is mythopoeic. The early Greek belief in the anthropomorphic gods who controlled events is an example. A cosmology is a set of basic and fundamental conceptions in terms of which all aspects of the experienced physical world can be understood. The conceptions include contingency, necessity, time, space, extension, magnitude, number, motion, change, quality, matter, force, causality, etc.[26] Moving from a cosmogony to a cosmology corresponds to the shift from primitive mind to logical mind, in Levy-Bruhl's typology,[27] or to participation in the worldwide movement to a higher level of civilization, in Jasper's suggested "axial age."[28]

Perhaps even more important than the shift from cosmogony to cosmology was the development of a single, generally accepted cosmology. The comparison with the parallel development in India is instructive. The ancient Indian literature contains cosmogonies. In the Rg Veda creation is said to have occurred when the father, who was embracing his daughter, the Dawn, was struck by an arrow from the bow of his son, the Skilled Archer, and withdrawing spilled his semen upon the highest peak of the Earth, at the place of Sacrifice.[29] In the Chandogya Upanishad the creation of the earth is said to have occurred through the development of a cosmic egg, which after the period of a year split asunder into a silver half and a golden half, the silver becoming the earth; the gold, the sky; the outer membrane, the mountains; the inner membrane, clouds and mist; the veins, rivers, the fluid within, the ocean.[30] When the six great systems of Hinduism were developed, cosmologies replaced cosmogonies, but each system developed its own cosmology and for hundreds of years these cosmologies flourished side by side together with other cosmologies from Buddhism, Jainism, and Carvakian materialism.[31]

Why was Indian civilization content with a variety of truths about the physical universe, when Western civilization sought a single truth? F. S. C. Northrop found the explanation in the form of the concepts used respectively by the Greeks and by the Indians to grasp and understand the physical universe. He said that Greeks used concepts by postulation the meaning of which is to be found not by direct reference to experience but in other concepts linked in an hierarchical system flowing from premises which are verified only indirectly by correspondence of deduced theorems with observed nature, whereas the Indians used concepts by intuition, the meaning of which is fully given by direct reference to experience.[32] The distinction is extremely useful for some purposes, but I believe it *expresses* the difference, rather than explaining it. Human beings are often duped by their own logical inventions, but I do not think that Greek adoption of universality as a characteristic of physical reality is an instance.

Another explanation arises from the perspective of the present investigation, namely, that human beings seek what they perceive to be life opportunities in the world as they understand it to be. The dominant opportunity open to the Indo-European people who migrated into the Greek peninsula was to change from a seminomadic life to fixed agriculture. In order to successfully exploit this opportunity it was necessary to learn how to control the physical world, and to organize human society on the basis of that knowledge. The families, gens, and city-states in which authority to make all important decisions was placed in those males who were believed to be best able to approach the gods was still the prevailing social order during the period of the presocratic philosophers. Living and working in such a cultural context conditioned the presocratics to assume that the external, material world was the significant reality. Is it not equally reasonable to suppose that the same conditioning would cause them to assume that the purpose of understanding the external, material world was to organize human cooperative efforts in ways that would effectively control the physical world to the benefit of human beings?

If this purpose was a part of the perspective of the presocratics they would have expected their understanding of the pertinent reality to yield an indication of the source of wise (in the sense of beneficial to the whole society) decisions. With respect to this matter the shift from the belief that local gods caused the animation and order in things to the search for causes within the physical nature of things was of profound significance. What was sought to be achieved was social organization and action consistent with and which effectively utilized physical events. The first step was to learn what physical events would occur or to cause desired events to occur. In the gods-cause-physical-events world the first step was sought to be accomplished by the auspices. In the natural-cause-and-effect world the first step was sought to be accomplished by learning what was irreducible and ultimate and how that part of reality caused gross objects and physical events.

The second step in achieving social organization and action consistent with and which effectively utilized physical events was to distribute the making of important decisions to those who appeared to be best able to learn what events would occur or best able to induce or cause favorable events to occur. In the gods-cause-physical-events world the second step was sought to be accomplished by the social order of the patriarchal family and the city-state which replicated the structure of that family. In the natural-cause-and-effect world, the second step was not yet contemplated at the time of the presocratics. It was Socrates who focused attention upon the knower of the natural-cause-and-effect world.[33] Plato and Aristotle believed that only the few could know causes of events and, therefore, only the few should be allowed to govern.[34] The Stoics believed that every mature human being was capable of learning about causes and effects and therefore all were equal in their capacity to make important decisions. Immense changes in social organization and in the legal system flowed from general acceptance of the Stoic view.

The point I wish to make at the moment is that the Greek natural philosophers adopted a single set of canons of argument and participated in the search for a single version of truth about the physical universe because they assumed that the truth about the physical world was the first step towards accomplishing that which was most desired, namely, the effective control of physical events. For this purpose, social organization and action could not be based on a number of different contradictory understandings of the physical world; there had to be a single generally accepted truth. This explains the pursuit of a single cosmology in the West. Beneficial control of the physical world was not viewed as the dominant life opportunity by the Indians and therefore the external, material world was not the most significant reality for them and toleration of contradictory cosmologies did not impede the pursuit of what the Indians most desired.

The explanation of the Western pursuit of a single cosmology is not sufficient, however, to explain universality as a characteristic of reality. It is possible to have a single, generally accepted cosmology which does not specify a single universal source of things and events, but many sources. The view that various gods caused physical events was generally believed throughout the Hellenic world; and therefore the sources of events were many. The cosmology that evolved from the work of the presocratics specified a single, universal source of things and of physical events— natural causes. The divinity that caused rain to fall in Athens might not be the same as the divinity that caused rain to fall in Sparta, or Delos, or Rhodes. But matter, space, number, and change were everywhere the same and natural philosophers from Miletus, Colophon, Ephesus, Samos, Croton, Elea, Acragas, Clazomenae, Abdera, and Athens could contribute over a period of one hundred and fifty years to working out the atomic theory in answer to Thales' question, How can we account for the changing world around us?[35]

The Characteristic of Objectivity

Parmenides had immense influence on the effort of the presocratics to understand reality because his reasoning initiated the canons of thought that made it possible for many persons, over several generations, to participate in a cumulative systematic investigation of the nature of the physical world. The Ionians had said that everything is composed of primal bits of sensible matter. The Pythagoreans had said that everything is composed of numerical material units created when form acting as limit imposed order on inchoate matter from the void. Heraclitus had sought to understand the relative stability of observed objects in view of the constant change of everything into its opposite. Were all of these views true? Or none? Was it necessary to establish that a view was true, or was personal preference sufficient? If truth was needed, what was the standard of proof? Was truth established by consistency with observed phenomena of the sensible world?

The outcome of the response to Parmenides' poem was that the presocratics adopted the position, subsequently expounded so eloquently and profoundly by Plato, that personal preference is to be rejected in favor of truth, and that observations of the sensible world can not yield truth but reasoning can.[36] The structure of Parmenides' poem reflects these two positions. It is divided into two parts, following the proem. In the first part, The Way of Truth, Parmenides deduces the characteristics of reality from the statement of existence—what it means to say that something *is*. In the second part, called The Way of Seeming, he sets out the positions resulting from observations of nature. With complete confidence, Parmenides asserts that any and all of these positions are false if they are inconsistent with deductions from the statement of existence.

Parmenides included among the false positions based on observations of nature the assertions of "being and not being," and of "coming into being and perishing." In the sections above on The Characteristic of Noncontradiction and The Characteristic of Being, I have set out the reasoning that shows, respectively, that being and not being, and coming into being and perishing, are inconsistent with the logical implications of the statement that "What is, is." Parmenides also calls false the assertion of "change of place." The reasoning is as follows: If stuff is and nothing else is, there is no place where stuff is not. Therefore, it is logically impossible for any stuff to move from one place to another.

By showing that being and not being are logically inconsistent, Parmenides demonstrated that if the Ionian position that matter is ultimate and irreducible is true, the Pythagorean assertion of a void can not be true. By showing that coming into being and perishing and change of place are logically inconsistent with the position that stuff is and nothing but stuff is, Parmenides demonstrated that if the Ionian position is true, the position of Heraclitus that change is constantly occurring can not be true. This follows because change can occur in only two ways, by generation, or by movement. Change by generation is ruled out if coming into being and perishing is logically impossible. Change by movement is ruled out if it is logically impossible for any of the presently existing stuff to move because there is no place where stuff is not.

Parmenides concluded that the universe is a solid, uniform sphere, rigid and motionless. This view was not fruitful and was rather quickly rejected. But that is of not particular significance. Parmenides is important because he initiated the canons of thought for relating abstract concepts to each other. The general acceptance of these canons by the presocratics and their full development by Plato and Aristotle entailed the acceptance of objectivity as a characteristic of reality in Western civilization. The physical world is what it is independent of the wishes or perceptions of human beings.

How the Real is Known

General acceptance of the canons of thought initiated by Parmenides not only entailed acceptance of objectivity as a characteristic of reality, it also set the pattern for the distinctive epistemology of Western civilization, with its indirect way of knowing reality. In expounding the Way of Truth, Parmenides reasons dialectically, that is, without reference to observed experience. He uses canons of reasoning to determine what it means to say that something *is*. The dependence upon abstract concepts and a logic that can conclusively establish the correctness or incorrectness of asserted relationships between such concepts is the beginning of an epistemology that eventually evolved into modern science.

In modern science conclusive falsification is possible, but not conclusive verification. This results from the indirect way of knowing a real material world that gives rise to the world of appearance. A set of abstract concepts are hypothesized to fully and completely state, in the most summary form, the nature of physical reality. Implications of these premises are deduced, and the resulting theorems are experimentally checked against observed nature. For instance a light wave of the frequency which theoretically falls within the blue part of the spectrum of light visible to the human eye is generated. If an observer with normal color vision sees a blue light the theorem is verified, but the premises from which the theorem is deduced are not verified. All possible theorems would have to be proved in order to conclusively verify the premises. Therefore, all that can be said after any number of positive experimental results is that the theory represented by the set of premises has not been falsified. If, however, any one experiment proves a theorem false, the set of premises from which it was deduced is also conclusively shown to be false, because the set of premises is supposed to state the truth in all instances.[37]

The Greeks at their best, including Plato and Aristotle, were never able to test abstract concepts and theories experimentally. They tested them dialectically. That is, they tested them against each other, and against common sense. Parmenides was not able to verify the Ionian view that the physical world is composed of primal bits of matter. What he did conclusively prove was that *if* matter exists, and *if* nothing else exists, then change is logically impossible—for the reasons indicated above. Of course dialectical reasoning left some choices to be made that could only be based on practical judgment. If the Ionian position, carried to its full logical implication, required the conclusion that change is impossible, and yet so much perceived experience indicated that change occurs, and the Heraclitean theory posited change as primary, several alternatives were possible: (1) Hold that materiality is real and perceived change is illusory; (2) Hold that change is real and materiality is illusory; (3) Seek some new theory that would account for both materiality and change within the real world. The modern scientific method of testing theories results in conclusive falsification if the experimental result is negative. The earlier dialectical method results in only contingent falsification. In both cases, however, the result is to set investigators searching for a new, more adequate theory.

The result of the indirect method of verification of theories of reality was that while the West has tended to hold a single generally accepted theory at any given time, a number of different theories have been adhered to serially as one is conclusively or contingently falsified and new theories compete until one comes to be generally accepted as true because it has, to that point, survived attempts to prove it false. Parmenides initiated the dialectical method of contingent falsification that resulted in the process of rejection and competitive supersession of theories. Two schools of philosophers adopted opposing sides of a dualism and vied for acceptance of their respective positions until both positions were shown to lead to inconsistency or absurdity and a third school came forward with a new set of premises that solved in a different way the problem to which the two positions of the dualism had been proposed as the answer. The theory of the third school would then hold the field until in turn it was contingently falsified. Bertrand Russell said that this see-saw process among the presocratics gave Hegel the ideal for his concept of the dialectic.[38] The use of abstract, indirectly verified concepts, with the entailed process of periodic contingent falsification and competitive supersession, drew Western philosophers step by step into an understanding of reality that was profoundly different from anything in ancient India or ancient China.

Notes

1. F.S.C. Northrop, *Science and First Principles* (New York, N.Y.: Macmillan, 1931), p. 3.
2. Bertrand Russell, *The Wisdom of the West*, ed. Paul Foulkes (London: Macdonald & Co., 1959), pp. 44–45.
3. Jose Ortega y Gasset, *Concord and Liberty*, trans. Helen Weyl (New York, N.Y.: W. W. Norton, 1946), pp. 66–67.
4. Gregory Vlastos, *Plato's Universe* (Seattle: University of Washington Press, 1975), p. xii. The Greeks did not discover what we now mean by ''science,''

but they discovered the conception of the universe that is presupposed by modern science.

5. Gerald Holton, "The Mainsprings of Discovery," in *The Nature of Scientific Discovery*, ed. Owen Gingerich (Washington, D.C.: Smithsonian, 1975); Gerald Holton, "The Thematic Imagination in Science," in *Science and Culture: A Study of Cohesive and Disjunctive Forces*, ed. Gerald Holton (Boston: Houghton Mifflin, 1965), pp. 88–108.

6. G. S. Kirk and J. E. Raven, *The Presocratic Philosophers* (Cambridge: Cambridge Univ. Press, 1966), pp. 107–110. Anaximander, a Milesian only a few years younger than Thales, proposed "The Unbounded."

7. Ibid., pp. 324, 367.

8. W. K. C. Gunthrie, *The Greek Philosophers: From Thales to Aristotle* (New York, N.Y.: Harper & Row, 1960), p. 41; Plato, *Symposium*, pp. 186–187 (standard pagination).

9. Bertrand Russell, *The Wisdom of the West*, ed. Paul Foulkes (London: Macdonald and Co., 1959), p. 22.

10. Kirk and Raven, p. 256.

11. Aristotle, *Metaphysics*, 13: 8. Later Pythagoreans, however, went far towards developing the theory of ideas, which was fully developed by Socrates and Plato, under which the form of a triangle, or any figure, is an abstract idea, devoid of substance and existing in the intelligible world instead of the sensible world. Plato, *Republic*, 5: 472–473 and 6: 509–513, *Timaeus*, pp. 28–29, *Phaedo*, pp. 78–79, *Phaedrus*, p. 247.

12. Kirk and Raven, pp. 187–197.

13. James A. Beattie, "Water," *Encyclopedia Britannica* (Chicago: Encyclopedia Britannica, 1970), 23: 270–271; Lyle T. Alexander, "Chemical Properties of Soil" sec. 5 of "Soil," 20: 837–840; James B. Parsons, "Elements, Chemical," 8: 270–273.

14. Gunther von Elbe, "Combustion," Ibid., 6: 126–128.

15. Plato, *Theaetetus*, pp. 178–182.

16. Russell, p. 28.

17. Kirk and Raven, p. 271.

18. Lucien Levy-Bruhl, *How Natives Think*, trans. Lilian A. Clare (New York, N.Y.: A. Knopf, 1926), pp. 105–136.

19. The rule of equitable estoppel.

20. Parmenides was expounding all the implications of being in the first part of his poem. In this sense, what I am discussing herein is the characteristic of constancy. I use "being" in speaking of this aspect of reality in order to distinguish the position that some part of reality is caused by generation. See Aristotle, *On Generation and Corruption*, 1.2.

21. Plato, *Theaetetus*, p. 152.

22. Kirk and Raven, p. 273.

23. Horace S. Thayer, ed., *Newton's Philosophy of Nature* (New York, N.Y.: Hafner, 1953, 1960), pp. 9–26.

24. F. S. C. Northrop, *The Meeting of East and West* (New York, N.Y.: Macmillan, 1946), pp. 197–199.

25. St. Louis Post-Dispatch, June 19, 1976. A front page story reported that thirty-five physicists at Stanford and the University of California (Berkeley) had announced the discovery of a property of matter called "charm." Previously discovered properties of subatomic matter called "quarks," are particles, and the property called "strangeness" resembles an electrical charge.

26. Francis MacD. Cornford, trans., *Plato's Cosmology: The Timaeus of Plato* (New York, N.Y.: Bobbs-Merrill, n.d.), p. 31; Milton K. Munitz, "Cosmology," *Encyclopedia of Philosophy*, ed. Paul Edwards (New York, N.Y.: Macmillan (The Free Press, 1967), 2: 237–244.

27. See above, p. 22.

28. Karl Jaspers, *The Origin and Goal of History,* trans. Michael Bullock (New Haven, CT: Yale Univ. Press, 1953).

29. Stella Kramrisch, "Natural Science and Technology in Relation to Cultural Patterns and Social Practices in India," in *Philosophy and Culture East and West,* ed. C. A. Moore (Honolulu: Univ. of Hawaii Press, 1961), p. 159.

30. S. Radhakrishnan and C. A. Moore, *A Source Book in Indian Philosophy* (Princeton: Princeton Univ. Press, 1957), p. 65.

31. S. Chatterjee and D. M. Datta, *An Introduction to Indian Philosophy,* fifth ed., (Calcutta: Univ. of Calcutta, 1954), pp. 9–10.

32. Northrop, *East and West,* pp. 447–450; Northrop, *Logic of the Sciences and the Humanities* (New York, N.Y.: Macmillan, 1947), pp. 77–101; Northrop, "The Relation Between Naturalistic Scientific Knowledge and Humanistic Intrinsic Values in Western Culture," in *Contemporary American Philosophy,* ed. J. E. Smith (London: George Allen & Unwin, 1970), pp. 107–151.

33. Plato, *Apology,* pp. 28–31; Plato, *Phaedo,* pp. 96–99.

34. Plato, *Statesman,* pp. 300–303; Plato, *Republic,* 3–4; Aristotle, *Politics,* 3. 7, 4. 6, 7; Aristotle, *Ethics* 8. 11.

35. Russell, pp. 44–45.

36. Plato, *Cratylus,* pp. 439–440; Plato, *Phaedrus,* pp. 249–250; Plato, *Phaedo,* pp. 78–80; Plato, *Theaetetus,* p. 186.

37. Holton, "Thematic Imagination," pp. 88–108; Northrop, *Logic,* pp. 119–132.

38. Russell, p. 15.

4

Plato

The respective answers given to the question of whether the 'Real' is one or many were decisive in establishing a basic difference between Western civilization and the civilizations of India and China. In the latter two instances the answer was that the real is an undivided one. The observed differentiations—animals, plants, people, soil, rivers, the sea—are predicated of the one reality, rather than being discrete entities possessing predicates of their own and each properly the object of study directed to understanding what it is, rather than its place and function in the universe. Of course, it is necessary to return, once more, to the point that Western civilization took the external, material world as the significant reality, and the Indian and Chinese civilizations did not. For the Indians and the Chinese the answer that the real is an undivided one was satisfactory because they did not need to depend upon understanding and controlling the physical world in order to achieve what they most desired. Being able to stay with the position that the real is an undivided one enabled them to avoid the contradictions that drove the presocratics to make the distinction, which became the hallmark of Western civilization, between the real world known rationally, and the apparent world known by the senses.

The ascription of being caused the Greeks to think of determinate entities as objects, having predicates of their own, leading to Aristotle's empirical study and classification of biological genera and species. Plato tells us that Protagoras, Heraclitus, Empedocles, and all the other presocratics except Parmenides held the position that all things are always in motion, that is, that nothing *is*, but is constantly in the process of becoming other than what it momentarily is.[1] Plato speaks of entities possessed of being as "self-existent things," and he says that with regard to that which is constantly becoming "we are not to allow either the word 'something,' 'belonging to something,' or 'to me,' or 'this' or 'that,' or any other detaining name to be used.''[2]

If all things are constantly becoming, the real is a many. That is, there is no one thing possessed of being which always remains the same and which combines to constitute all other things. Preeminent among those who held that the real is a many were the Pythagoreans, who were critical of Parmenides' cosmology of a solid uniform sphere, rigid and motionless. Zeno of Elea, a disciple of Parmenides and the first great practitioner of the dialectical method of reasoning, set out to show the inconsistencies in the Pythagorean cosmology.

Zeno asked two questions. Both seemed to require an affirmative answer, yet it was impossible for both affirmative answers to be correct. One question was whether units have magnitude. In the Pythagorean cosmology all matter and gross objects are composed of combinations of units. A line is composed of a series of units. This makes sense because the real is material. A unit is an irreducible, indivisible bit of stuff. Everything else in the world is composed of such units. Therefore, the answer to this question had to be affirmative. If units did not have magnitude even an infinite number of them could not compose a line. The other question Zeno asked was whether any magnitude can be divided. The key to the importance of this question is whether *any* magnitude can be divided. It is a perfectly good logical proposition, formally proved in Euclid's Book X, Proposition 1, that if two lines of unequal magnitude are set out and from the greater a magnitude greater than its half is subtracted, and this process is repeated continually, there will be left some magnitude which will be less than the lesser magnitude set out. This means that any magnitude is infinitely divisible; that there is no smallest magnitude, because there will always be some smaller magnitude. However, infinite divisibility could not be applied to the experienced world of material substance. A very small bit of matter, a Pythagorean unit, being infinitely divided would cease to have any magnitude, and the matter and gross objects of the physical world could not exist. Thus Zeno succeeded in discrediting the Pythagorean cosmology by showing that its concept of unit was incompatible with infinite divisibility which was a perfectly valid, logical proposition and which was needed in certain mathematical calculations.[3]

Parmenides was held in awe and reverence by Socrates, presumably for his contribution to the understanding of being.[4] Parmenides held that the real is an undivided one, but he rejected the concept of space. As a result his universe was a solid uniform sphere, rigid and motionless. Change could not occur. Instead of leading to an understanding of physical causes and effects, this view denies them, and therefore was clearly unsatisfactory for the purpose of ordering human society in ways that would effectively utilize physical events.

The resolving, superseding third position, between the extremes of the one and the infinitely divisible many, was stated by Leucippus. He suggested the existence of atomic particles, infinite in number but irreducible in magnitude, and he revived the notion of the void, or empty space, in which the atoms were constantly moving. The atomic theory is usually associated with the name of Democritus of Abdera, who flourished about 420 B.C. Democritus further developed the atomic theory and distinguished between the real world, which is composed of space and atoms in motion, and the world as human beings observe it, which he called the world of appearance. Democritus made the distinction in order to explain the incommensurability of certain magnitudes. The explanation was completely unsatisfactory but the distinction was intrinsically important and has remained a hallmark of Western systematic thought.

The discovery of incommensurable magnitudes was another of the contingent falsifications of current theory that drove Western philosophers further from the observed world into more profound discoveries about the world knowable only by indirectly verifiable abstract concepts. The discovery was that in certain triangles the lengths of the sides and of the hypotenuse cannot all be expressed in whole numbers, no matter what the unit of measure adopted. For instance in the right-angled triangle having a base of 1 and a hypotenuse of 2, the vertical side is the square root of 3; and in the right-angled triangle having a base of 1 and vertical side of 1, the hypotenuse is the square root of 2. This discovery forced the Greeks to give up the atomic theory, and it was not taken up again until modern times.

Why did the Greeks take the discovery of incommensurable magnitudes so seriously? The Chinese were aware of the incommensurability of the sides and the hypotenuse of some triangles and it bothered them not a whit. In fact the Chinese made important use in surveying and architecture of certain right-angled triangles in which the hypotenuse could not be expressed as a whole number. The incommensurable triangles that were important for the Chinese are: $5^2 + 5^2 = 7^2 (+1)$; $8^2 + 9^2 = 12^2 (+1)$; $8^2 + 4^2 = 9^2 (-1)$; and $7^2 + 4^2 = 8^2 (+1)$.[5] Notice that in each case the square of the hypotenuse is plus or minus one the square of a whole number. It was this play of the number one, or unity, that made these incommensurable triangles useful to the Chinese.

Neither the Chinese nor the presocratics had generalized the concept of number. For both, number referred to reality. But, of course, the realities were different. For the Greeks, number referred to a material, nondivisible particle, or to a concrete magnitude composed of such atomic particles.

For the Chinese, number referred to a normative geometric and sequential ordering of observed phenomena.[6] The Chinese emperor functioned as the gnomon which enabled the order of Heaven to flow into the creatures and events of the Earth, putting them in the correct geometrical and sequential order. Earth represented by the square and Heaven represented by the circle were joined by the upright gnomon. Chariots, buildings, and cities were constructed to symbolically represent due proportion and the normative connection between Heaven and Earth. The actual height of the current emperor was used, together with the appropriate incommensurable triangle, as the measure of all constructions; but through the play of the one in the incommensurable triangles (which was not counted because it represented the play of "Unity which is not reckoned but which is equal to and creates the whole," because it symbolized the function of the emperor as the central gnomon connecting Heaven and Earth) the dimensions were kept always the same.[7]

Since the Chinese used numbers primarily as symbolic indicators of normative geometric and sequential ordering of phenomena, the incommensurability of the sides and hypotenuses of some triangles did not present any difficulty. The symbolic meaning of the emperor as gnomon enabled surveyors and architects to adjust the actual dimensions of constructions to the normative dimensions of the universe. But for the Greeks number referred to segments and particles of physical matter. Atomic particles in a series composed a line; lines combined to form gross objects. Acceptance of the atomic theory had entailed rejection of infinite divisibility. Atomic particles could not be cut. Numbers referred to such particles. Therefore every line must be composed of a whole number of particles. This is why the discovery of incommensurable magnitudes contingently falsified the atomic theory and required a new theory that would account for the incommensurability.

Democritus attempted to explain incommensurability without giving up the atomic theory by distinguishing between the real world and the world of appearance. He said that incommensurability was only in the world of appearance, thus attempting to save the atomic theory which referred to the real world. This distinction fixed in the heritage of Western civilization an extremely important characteristic, but it was an unsatisfactory attempt to meet the devastating effect of incommensurable magnitudes upon the atomic theory. The later Pythagoreans had begun to develop the theory of ideas, which was adopted and fully developed by Socrates and Plato. The theory of ideas was the coming to self-consciousness about the fact that concepts are abstract. A concept such as "triangle" was not any particular, concrete configuration with two sides and a hypotenuse, but it was the abstract idea of such configurations. The distinction proposed by Democritus had the effect of classifying commensurable triangles as ideas but incommensurable triangles as particular, concrete, observed phenomena. This was unsound. A triangle with sides of 1, 1 and the square root of 2 is just as much a concept, an idea, as a triangle with sides of 3, 4, and 5.

Plato solved the problem of incommensurable magnitudes, but he did more than that. He established the distinction between the real, indirectly known, world, and the world known by the senses as a permanent characteristic of Western civilization, and he established the primacy of order in understanding both of these worlds.

In the hundred and fifty years between Thales and Democritus the presocratics tended to investigate the nature of things and neglect the nature of animation and order. Probably the Ionians assumed that the primal stuff was alive—the animating and ordering power having moved from external gods into the earth, or water, etc.—and therefore capable of causing the motion of itself and all things which it composed.[8] It is clear, however, that Democritean atoms are solid bits of matter in all shapes and sizes which are in constant motion in empty space. In the absence of modern scientific theories about the combination of atoms into molecules, cells, and crystals, and the laws of gravity, electromagnetics, and strong and weak interactions, what could explain the combination of Democritean atoms into earth, air, fire, and water, and into the myriad creatures and things of the universe? Nothing remained to explain animation, and the atomists did not explain it. They simply asserted that atoms were in constant motion. The only explanation of order was the chance coming together of atoms and the assertion that like tends towards like.

Plato's treatment of order is so powerful and intellectually rich that it left a permanent impress on Western civilization. His treatment of animation, on the other hand, is weak and proved to be a major point at which Aristotle attacked the theory of his former teacher. It was not open to Plato to develop a mechanistic account of causes and effects such as the modern world was taught to expect by Galileo, Descartes, Newton, and the industrial revolution. The ancients did not know machines, they knew only tools. Machines are driven by their own power and, to a significant extent, are controlled by their own devices; the action of one part is caused by another part acting upon it. Tools do not themselves cause anything, but are only the means by which the skill and intelligence of the user can achieve a desired end.[9] Plato understood order as intelligence, design, reason.

Plato asserted and developed full and detailed chains of reasoning to support the assertion that a single, noncontradictory, eternal, universal, objective order exists throughout every aspect of the cosmos, from the tiniest microcosm to the great orbits of the stars. Action in accordance with that order is good. Thought in accordance with that order is true. Structure in accordance with that order is beautiful.

The atomists held that the indivisible atoms were of an infinite variety of shapes and sizes and a material world was formed when a vortex occurred as the atoms drifted in the void. Whirling about and bumping into each other, atoms sometimes stuck together because they were of like nature or were "congruent." For instance, heavy atoms would drift together and light atoms would drift together, and a hook-shaped atom might catch onto an eye-shaped atom.[10] In this way all material things came into existence. Atomists assumed that innumerable worlds had been formed and then had disintegrated under the impact of subsequent vortices. In such a world there is necessity, in the sense of immediate causes such as bumping, being bumped, or catching onto another atom, but this kind of necessity is not to be understood in the sense of natural cause and effect of the masses and velocities in a Newtonian world, for instance. In Plato's time necessity was associated with accident, coincidence, chance or spontaneity.[11] A world formed by Democritean atoms whirling and bumping about until they stuck to each other would have an order, but it would be meaningless to speak of standards of truth, goodness, or beauty. Further, as the atomists themselves foresaw, a world created by chance can be destroyed by chance.

Plato assumed that there was only one visible, tangible world—the world that human beings live in—and he wanted to develop a theory that would account for the continuing existence of that world. This presented something of a difficulty because of Plato's position that nothing in the visible world had being; everything is constantly coming to be. Parmenides had taught Greek philosophers the implications of being. "What is, is." Being exists. That which is not being does not exist. Plato found a way to bring becoming into the realm of existence by pointing out that "is" can mean "exists" or it can mean "the same as." Then "what is not" can mean "does not exist" or "is different from." Since the intelligible world is composed of incorporeal forms which have being, it is eternal, unchanging, universal. The visible world, composed of material objects which are constantly becoming, is not nonexistent, but it is different from the intelligible world in that everything is coming into being and passing out of being, and therefore is constantly changing, and this process occurs in time and space. In order to speak meaningfully of the continued existence of the visible world it is necessary to define the nature of the visible world, or the cosmos, and Plato does this in his mythical account of the creation of the world by the god, or demiurge.

Plato's solution to the problem of the one and the many is crucial to his account of both the intelligible world and the visible world. He did not restrict himself to choosing between the alternatives of the one or the many. His solution was the one *and* the many. Implications of this position make the Western view of reality significantly different from that of Indian or Chinese civilization. However, the position that the one *and* the many are real immediately raises the question of the relationship between the one and the many, which has remained a central concern of Western philosophy and, even more so, Western theology.

The position of Indian and Chinese civilizations that the real is one avoids the problems of the relationship between the one and the many because the relationship is one of identity. The whole of reality is a unity; and subclassifications refer not to discrete entities, but to differentiations of the one. Nothing short of the entire universe, or the undifferentiated continuum, has being. Everything else is a transitory attribute of the one. An attribute is significant only in relation to that which it qualifies. Therefore, the natural question to ask when investigating an attribute is not What is it? but What does it do for (or what does it owe to) the thing it qualifies. Consequently, "the real is one" is an unsatisfactory position if the purpose of systematic investigation is to understand and control physical events, because every effect has to be traced back to a single, ultimate cause. It is a little like trying to understand animal husbandry in terms of the origin of the solar system. What is needed is some fixed point of reference a little closer to the effects sought to be understood, such as the invariant rules of transmission of genetic characteristics by genes which will yield implications for breeding animals with desired characteristics. Of course, discovery of the foundations of the science of genetics was the work of Mendel in the nineteenth century, but the Greeks set Western civilization on the course that led to this aspect, and to other aspects, of modern science when it began to ask What is it? of things other than the whole universe.

On the other hand, the position of the atomists that the real is a many is also unsatisfactory for the purpose of understanding and controlling physical events because if the real is a many, neither the structure nor the continued existence of any material world is predictable. It is not sufficient to discover invariant properties of entities. Predictability requires, in addition, invariant relationships between entities, and invariant structure in the whole universe. There is nothing for the kind of systematic investigation that eventually became modern Western science to lay hold of if Democritus is correct and innumerable worlds coalesce and disperse as the result of the accidental bumping and whirling about of atoms. In his account of the creation of the cosmos Plato deals first of all with the creation of one world and with binding this world together so it will not disintegrate.[12]

Plato's forms are not logical abstractions from objects whose real existence is in the sensible world. This is the Aristotelian view. Plato's forms exist as "living creatures" in the world known only by rational thought. The relationship between the one and the many is indicated in the passage of the *Timaeus* in which Plato begins his description of the creation of the cosmos—that is the earth, sun, moon, planets, and fixed stars. In order to account for the creation of the cosmos Plato introduces into Western philosophy[13] a creator god. The god is more accurately called a demiurge, or craftsman, because the unchanging forms of the intelligible world and the inchoate matter of the visible world are not created. What the demiurge creates is the order of the visible world.

Contrary to the jealous gods of Olympus who punished human beings for daring to aspire to the perfection of the gods, Plato's god desired that everything in the visible world should be, as nearly as possible, good and perfect. This being premised, Plato continues, at line 30c:

> What was the living creature in whose likeness he framed the world? We must not suppose that it was any creature that ranks only as a species; for no copy of that which is incomplete can ever be good. Let us rather say that the world is like, above all to that Living Creature of which all other living creatures, severally and in their families, are parts. For that embraces and contains within itself all the intelligible living creatures, just as this world contains ourselves and all other creatures that have been formed as things visible. For the god, wishing to make this world most nearly like that intelligible thing which is best and in every way complete, fashioned it as a single visible living creature, containing within itself all living things whose nature is of the same order.[14]

The difficulty with this passage, of course, is that Plato is using an image from common sense experience to explain the nature of something outside experience. Living creatures are experienced as corporeal; yet Plato is explaining the nature of something he asserts is incorporeal. Nevertheless, it is clear that Plato is rejecting both the position that only the one exists and the position that only the many exist. Calling the one and the many living creatures clearly indicates that each many is a complete whole, not just a part of something, and that all of the manys constitute a unity, which is also a complete whole. (The difficulty of thinking of incorporeal forms as living creatures doubtless explains why Christian theology uses anthropomorphic images of beings which are said to be incorporeal.)

In the *Sophist*, principally, but also in the *Phaedrus*, the *Phaedo*, the *Theaetetus*, and the *Republic*, we learn more about Plato's forms. The forms can not pass into the visible world, but they can "participate" with other forms in the composite form that is the ideal model for a type of flower, tree, bird, or animal in the visible world. Nothing is beautiful, or in motion, or exists, except as the pure form of beauty, motion, or existence participates in the composite form of which the visible object is a copy. Some of the forms are capable of blending or combining. Others are not. For instance, the form of motion is incapable of combining with the form of rest. Knowing how to take a synoptic view of many kinds of forms in order to be able to intuit the single generic form which participates in each, and knowing how to divide the generic form according to its natural articulations into the forms of species, is the science of dialectic, which yields true knowledge.

Plato says that the "business of the dialectical science" is "the division according to classes, which neither makes the same other, nor makes the other the same." He continues:

> Then, surely, he who can divide rightly is able to see clearly one form pervading a scattered multitude, and many different forms contained under one higher form; and again *one* form knit together into a single whole and pervading many such wholes, and many forms, existing only in separation and isolation.[15]

The precise nature of the relationships between Plato's forms is a very difficult matter that is the subject of much debate by specialists. It is clear, however, that a fixed order between the generic form and all the forms of species is a part of the ontology of Plato's absolute, unchanging intelligible world. To correctly collect species forms into a generic form, and to correctly divide a generic form into species forms, is to lay hold of truth.

Plato's science of dialectics consists of correctly identifying forms as the same or different. The form of the Same, and the form of the Different, pervade all other forms and are capable of combining because every form is the same as itself and different from any other. The form of Existence also pervades every other form. It is this trinity, Existence, Sameness and Difference, that Plato employs as the link between the intelligible world of pure forms and the visible world.

The first work of the creator god was to create the soul of the world. Soul is the source of animation and order. Animation occurs only in the visible world; the intelligible world is unchanging. Order, which is the product of rational intelligence, depends upon cognition that unfailingly grasps truth. Since the order of the world of forms must be copied in the visible world, the soul of the world needs an intelligence capable of knowing the truth in both worlds. The god, therefore, took as ingredients of the world soul some of the "indivisible and unchangeable," and some of "that which is divisible and has to do with material bodies," and he compounded an Intermediate Existence "partaking of the nature of the same and of the other."[16] The cognitive function consists of correctly identifying the Same and the Different. Therefore, the god compounded an Intermediate Sameness from Indivisible and Divisible Sameness, and an Intermediate Difference from Indivisible and Divisible Difference. He then mixed Intermediate Existence, Intermediate Sameness, and Intermediate Difference to form the soul of the world.

The structure of the intelligible world is known by rational intelligence through the science of dialectic. Plato believed that rational intelligence was possessed by the world soul and by the souls of a few men. Rational cognition was essentially remembering. The world soul, and a part of each human soul, Plato believed, are immortal. At some time before being joined to a body every soul had known the forms and their structure. Therefore, the embodied soul—whether world or human—when it exercised rational intelligence, simply recognized, or remembered, what it had once known. This process did not depend in the least upon perception of sensible objects, and reasoning from perceptions to conceptions. This position appears more reasonable if it is kept in mind that Plato was strongly influenced by the mathematical tradition of the Pythagoreans, and that the pure forms are analogous to mathematical concepts in that they make no reference to material objects or even mental images. The amazing ability of the occasional mathematical prodigy to arrive by independent thought at a very early age at the concepts of algebra or calculus lends plausibility to Plato's view of rational intelligence.

It is extremely important to realize that the structure, the order, of the intelligible world is the pattern of relationships between the one and many. When Plato's god created the visible world, he copied the forms of the intelligible world, but also, in order to bind the discrete objects of the world together so that the Platonic world would not disintegrate like a Democritean world, the god *copied the structure of the Intelligible world.* In the visible world the relationship between two material copies of incorporeal forms, i.e., between two magnitudes, is expressed mathematically as a ratio. When that ratio is preserved as the relationship between a series of magnitudes, the relationship is one of proportion. Plato's creator god uses ratio and proportion to bind together the visible world.

The god created the world from primary bodies, and he wanted to bind the constituent bodies together in unity and concord so that internal disharmony would not cause it to disintegrate. Without this unity and concord the perfection which the god desired would not be achieved. Plato's account of how the god achieved the desired internal perfection is as follows:

> Now that which comes to be must be bodily, and so visible and tangible; and nothing can be visible without fire, or tangible without something solid, and

nothing is solid without earth. Hence the god, when he began to put together the body of the universe, set about making it of fire and earth. But two things alone cannot be satisfactorily united without a third; for there must be some bond between them drawing them together. And of all bonds the best is that which makes itself and the terms it connects a unity in the fullest sense; and it is of the nature of a continued geometrical proportion to effect this most perfectly. For whenever, of three numbers, the middle one between any two that are either solids (cubes?) or squares, is such that, as the first is to it, so is it to the last, and conversely as the last is to the middle, so is the middle to the first, then since the middle becomes first and last, and again the last and first become middle, in that way all will necessarily come to play the same part towards one another, and by so doing they will all make a unity.

Now if it had been required that the body of the universe should be a plane surface with no depth, a single mean would have been enough to connect its companions and itself; but in fact the world was to be solid in form, and solids are always conjoined, not by one mean, but by two. Accordingly the god set water and air between fire and earth, and made them, so far as was possible, proportional to one another, so that as fire is to air, so is air to water, and as air is to water, so is water to earth, and thus he bound together the frame of a world visible and tangible.

For these reasons and from such constituents, four in number, the body of the universe was brought into being, coming into concord by means of proportion, and from these it acquired Amity, so that coming into unity with itself it became indissoluble by any other save him who bound it together.[17]

The result of using ratio and proportion to bind together the constituent parts of the world is to produce symmetry in the whole structure. Plato says, in the above quoted excerpt, that a "continued geometrical proportion" will effect unity most perfectly. He then states that the god established a continued (continuous) geometrical proportion between the four primary bodies, "so that as fire is to air, so is air to water, and as air is to water, so is water to earth." Plato indicates that two mean terms are needed to bind fire and earth because the world is not two-dimensional, but three-dimensional. This refers to the fact that if you take a root and set out the numbers produced by successive multiples, there will be one number between square numbers and two between cube numbers. For instance, set out the numbers resulting from:

2   (2×2) (4×2) (8×2) (16×2) (32×2)

The numbers are:

2   4   8   16   32   64

Four is a square number (2^2) and 16 is a square number (4^2). Between 4 and 16 there is only one number (mean), 8. Eight is a cube number $(2 \times 2) \times 2$, and the next cube number is 64 $(4 \times 4) \times 4$.[18] Between 8 and 64 there are two numbers (means), 16 and 32.

A cube number is compounded from three numbers, representing each of the dimensions of a solid body—length, width, and depth. The continuous geometrical proportion using three as the ratio between magnitudes, and beginning with unity, is: 1, 3, 9, 27. In what sense does such a continuous geometrical progression bind the terms of the progression into a unity? The terms are not mixed or blended together. Neither are they restricted or reduced to the unity of equality. There is, however, a unity of ratio. Ratio states the relationship between two magnitudes. The continuous proportion repeats the ratio between all other pairs of magnitudes in the set, thus making the relationship permanent and pervasive between the several parts and between parts and the whole. The relationship between parts and between parts and whole are all analogous, from *ana logon,* according to reason.[19]

The result of using a continuous geometrical proportion is a dynamic symmetry. In modern usage symmetry means a repetition of identical elements on each side of an axis. The dynamic symmetry which was the goal of Greek and Gothic architecture and Western art was consonance between elements that were not identical and between all of the elements and the whole.[20] This is the meaning of Plato's statement in the excerpt, *supra,* from the *Timaeus,* "the body of the universe was brought into being, coming into concord by means of proportion."[21] Vitruvius, who transmitted all we know of lost Greek treatises on architecture, writes:

> Symmetry resides in the correlation by measurement between the various elements of the plan, and between each of those elements and the whole. . . . As in the human body . . . it proceeds from proportion—the proportion which the Greeks called analogia—which achieves consonance between every part and the whole. . . . This symmetry is regulated by the *modulus,* the standard of common measure for the work considered, which the Greeks called "The Number." . . . When every important part of the building is thus conveniently set in proportion by the right correlation between height and width, between width and depth, and when all these parts have also their place in the total symmetry of the building, we obtain *eurythmy.*[22]

If Plato did have in mind the progression 1, 3, 9, 27, in speaking about the god placing the primary bodies of the world in geometrical proportion, the modulating number that would bring these primary bodies into concord and unity is 3. It seems likely that Plato did have in mind the continuous geometrical proportion based on the ratio 3, not only because it is appropriate for solid bodies but also because the god uses this ratio and the double ratio, based on 2, to make proportional divisions in the world soul.

Immediately after his account of the composition of world soul, from Intermediate Existence, Sameness, and Difference, Plato says:

> And having made a unity of the three, again he divided this whole into as many parts as was fitting, each part being a blend of Sameness, Difference, and Existence.
>
> And he began the division in this way. First he took one portion from the whole, and next a portion double of this; the third half as much again as the second, and three times the first; the fourth double of the second; the fifth three times the third; the sixth eight times the first; and the seventh twenty-seven times the first.[23]

The numbers resulting from the prescribed division are 1, 2, 3, 4, 8, 9, 27. That is a combination of the double and the triple continuous geometrical proportions, beginning with unity and taking the first even and the first odd number as the root and proceeding as far as the solid number. The double proportion is 1, 2, 4, 8. The triple proportion is 1, 3, 9, 27. The god then further divides world soul at intervals corresponding to arithmetic and harmonic proportions. The Pythagorean tradition of all the powers of the material world springing from unity; the Pythagorean tradition of order being imposed upon chaos by harmonic divisions of a tuned string; the Platonic concept of binding the primary bodies of the material world into unity by geometric proportion; and the Platonic concept of reproducing the structures of the intelligible world and the visible world in the soul of the world, all conduce to the conclusion that the two continuous geometrical proportions based on the ratio 2, the number appropriate for two-dimensional magnitudes, and the ratio 3, the number appropriate for three-dimensional magnitudes, are used as the primary divisions of world soul (and then arithmetic and harmonic divisions are added) in order to enable the world soul to apprehend every aspect of the structure of matter and of the material world.[24]

We have discussed the god's use of the continuous geometrical proportion based on the ratio of 3 to bind together the primary bodies into the unity and concord of dynamic symmetry, thus protecting the world against the disintegration of a Democritean world which had only accidental structure. Plato did not stop with binding material bodies into the stabilizing order of geometrical proportion. He went on to infuse order as a first principle into matter itself. Primary bodies, like everything else in the visible world, all of which is composed of primary bodies, were constantly coming to be. Out of what were Platonic primary bodies composed? The creator god did not create the unchanging forms of the intelligible world; and he also did not create but found ready to his hand the materials of the visible world—although in chaotic form. The powers of heat, cold, solidness, lightness, brightness, dryness, which are the sensible qualities of Platonic primary bodies, existed before the ordering action of the god but also in unordered and unbalanced agitation. The four kinds of primary bodies, in inchoate form, tended to drift together like Democritean atoms. Of this chaotic situation and the action of the god, Plato says:

> . . . the different kinds came to have different regions, even before the ordered whole consisting of them came to be. Before that, all these kinds were without proportion or measure. Fire, water, earth, and air possessed indeed some vestiges of their own nature, but were altogether in such a condition as we should expect for anything when deity is absent from it. Such being their nature at the time when ordering of the universe was taken in hand, the god then began by giving them a distinct configuration by means of shapes and numbers. That the god framed them with the greatest possible perfection, which they had not before, must be taken, above all, as a principle we constantly assert; what I must now attempt to explain to you is the distinct formation of each and its origin.[25]

When Plato begins his account of how the creator god brought the disordered powers of the inchoate primary bodies into an ordered whole by proportion and measure, we see why the continuous geometrical proportion, 1, 2, 4, 8, based on the ratio of 2, which is appropriate for two-dimensional magnitudes, was included with the continuous geometrical proportion, 1, 3, 9, 27, based on the ratio of 3 and appropriate for solid magnitudes, in the primary divisions of the world soul. Plato's primary bodies are solids, but he intends to generate them out of elementary plane surfaces.

Plato hypothesizes that the four primary bodies have the shape of four of the five regular solids, which were known to the Pythagoreans. "Regular" means that the surfaces of these solids are composed of plane surfaces of equal size, with equal sides and equal angles.[26] The way regular plane surfaces can be used to construct regular solids, and why there can be only five regular solids, can be easily understood if you cut out a number of the requisite plane figures from a sheet of paper and follow the brief description in the *Timaeus* or in Euclid XIII, 18. Begin with regular triangles. Place them flat on a table, move the apexes together, and imagine the apexes being lifted up and coming together so as to enclose a solid angle. Two equilateral triangles will not enclose a solid angle. Three will. A fourth will enclose the space between the bases of the first three, and you have the first of the regular solids, the tetrahedron, or pyramid. Try four regular triangles. You will find that they enclose a solid angle. Put four more together at the apexes and join the two sets at the bases and you have the next regular solid, the octahedron. Five regular triangles will also enclose a solid angle, and fifteen more will result in the icosahedron. No more solids can be formed from regular triangles because six apexes, each with a 60-degree angle, add up to the 360 degrees of a plane surface, and therefore the apexes can not be bent up to form a solid angle.

Now take some squares of equal size. Two will not enclose a solid angle. Three will. Add three more and you have the cube. Four squares, with their four right angles equalling 360 degrees, will not enclose a solid angle. Therefore, only one regular solid can be formed with square surfaces. Next take some pentagons (pentagons have equal angles and equal sides). Two will not enclose a solid angle. Three will. Add nine more and you have the fifth regular solid, the dodecahedron. Each angle of the pentagon being a right angle and a fifth, four of them equals more than 360 degrees and therefore cannot enclose a solid angle. And, as Euclid says, "Neither again will a solid angle be contained by other polygonal figures by reason of the same absurdity."[27] Therefore, only five regular solids can exist.

Plato reasoned that the most stable of the regular solids, the cube, is the shape of earth corpuscles. Of the remaining he assigned the pyramid to fire, because it was the smallest, most mobile, and had the sharpest angles, and the icosahedron to water because it was at the other end of the spectrum as to each of these attributes. The intermediate body, the octahedron, he assigned to air. The fifth regular solid, the dodecahedron, Plato assigned to the cosmos as a whole, by which he meant the earth, sun, moon, the planets, and the fixed stars—the whole visible universe—which he believed to have the shape of a sphere. The dodecahedron can easily become a sphere if the pentagonal surfaces are made of flexible material. There was a current custom of making balls from twelve pentagonal pieces of leather.[28]

The work of the creator god with respect to the primary bodies—and also with respect to the sun, moon, planets, and fixed stars, as we shall see—was to put the inchoate primary bodies into proportion so that their sensible powers could function in an orderly and therefore fully effective way. This was done by giving the primary bodies regular three-dimensional form, which was based on regular two-dimensional form. However, the regular two-dimensional forms, the equilateral, equiangular triangle, the square, and the pentagon, were not the atomic plane surfaces. These regular plane surfaces, in turn, were composed of atomic triangles.

The regular triangle, of which the tetrahedron, octahedron, and icosahedron are formed, is composed of right-angled scalene triangles. This enables Plato to provide a theoretical account of the transformation of fire,

air, and water into each other. For instance, six atomic triangles constituted one regular triangle. If three corpuscles of water were dispersed into
atomic triangles the result would be 360 atomic triangles (6 atomic triangles
$\times$ 20 regular triangular surfaces in the icosahedron $\times$ 3 water corpuscles).
These atomic triangles might recombine into five octahedral air corpuscles
(6 atomic triangles $\times$ 8 sides $\times$ 5 octahedrons = 240 atomic triangles) and
five corpuscles of fire (6 $\times$ 4 $\times$ 5 = 120). Atomic triangles also made it
possible to account theoretically for the assumed fact that earth, air, fire,
and water corpuscles came in different sizes or grades, which caused
(something like isotopes in present theory) differences in gross entities—
such as smaller air corpuscles composing the clear air of the upper
atmosphere and larger air corpuscles composing the dense and murky air
in glens and swamps. The square side of the cube is composed of right-
angled isosceles triangles.

The two atomic triangles which compose the four primary bodies have
the remarkable common characteristic of being arithmetically incommensurable. The right-angled scalene triangle has sides of 1, 2, and the square
root of 3. The right-angled isosceles triangle has sides of 1, and 1, and the
square root of 2. By using these triangles as the atoms of the material
world Plato has solved the problem of incommensurable magnitudes. He
has moved from arithmetical proportion, which states the relationships
between units, to geometrical proportion, which states the relationships
between two-dimensional plane magnitudes and between three-dimensional solid magnitudes. The sides of the triangle that are incommensurable
in units are commensurable "in the square." Arithmetical incommensurability is not cast out of the mathematical world as "mere appearance" but
is strikingly used to show that geometrical ratio is even more basic than
the atomic triangles. Thus geometrical proportion binds the four primary
bodies together in unity; geometrical proportion binds the atomic triangles
together into the unity of each of the four primary bodies; and geometrical
proportion is even prior to the atomic triangles, suggesting that the atomic
triangles if they were not physically generated by lines and lines by
numbers, after the Pythagorean tradition, at least are defined by geometrical proportion.

The pentagon is constructed from a different atomic triangle, the isosceles triangle having each of its base angles double of the vertical angle.[29]
In order to construct this atomic triangle it is necessary to divide a straight
line in what is called "extreme and mean ratio," which means that the
ratio of the whole to the greater part is the same as the ratio of the greater
part to the smaller part. The divisions of the line are arithmetically
incommensurable, but the ratio, which is 1.618, when used in continuous
geometrical proportion yields a most remarkable series. You will recall

that the series beginning with unity and using 2 and 3 as the ratios are, respectively, 1, 2, 4 (2 × 2), 8 (4 ×2), and 1, 3, 9 (3 × 3), 27 (9 × 3). Using 1.618 (usually designated as ø, which is pronounced phi) in the same way we get 1, 1.618 (ø), 2.618 (ø²), 4.236 (ø² × ø), and so on. In this infinite series each term is not only a multiple of phi, it is also the sum of the previous two terms in the series. In architecture this series permits volumes to be manipulated by simple addition and subtraction and produces dynamic symmetry with a minimum increase in scale at each geometric increment. Phi is the "golden section" ratio. It was known to the Pythagoreans and to the Egyptians, but Plato is said to have originated the theorems implied by it. The golden section is the ratio of the human body—between the total height and the distance from the navel to floor level and between other dimensions of the body. Indeed plants and animals quite generally follow the pentagonal geometrical proportions of the golden section, while the crystalline structure of the geosphere follows the arithmetical proportion of repeating identical units. The geometrical proportions based on the golden section ratio and closely related ratios clustered around the square root of 5 were used by Greek and medieval artists and architects to produce the dynamic symmetry of vases, paintings, sculpture, temples, and Gothic cathedrals.[30]

During ancient and medieval times the ratios and regulating diagrams for producing dynamic symmetry in buildings were jealously guarded secrets of the guilds of masons and stonecutters. When the reformation broke the monopoly of the Catholic masons, and Greek learning was revived in the renaissance, the secrets of the golden section, continuous geometrical proportion, and dynamic symmetry were published. Luca Pacioli in 1509 published a treatise, *Divina Proportione,* illustrated by Leonardo da Vinci, in which he discussed the superiority of the irrational, or geometrical, proportions over arithmetical proportions because the result was a dynamic symmetry.[31] Curiously, after the ratios and procedures for producing dynamic symmetry were no longer secret, the concept ceased to dominate architecture, although Palladio used the irrational proportions to produce dynamic symmetry; Christopher Wren's Sheldonian Theater in Oxford is a vertical modulation of the golden section; and Gabriel's facades on the Place de la Concorde are based on the golden section.[32] Among modern architects, Le Corbusier used a "modulor" based on the golden section ratio to achieve dynamic symmetry in his later buildings, including the chapel of Notre Dame du Haut at Ronchamp, but the modern symmetry of identical elements on each side of an axis has become dominant.[33]

The five regular solids are constructed by inscribing them within the sphere, which is symbolic of the spherical cosmos and also contains the irrational ratio of radius to circumference. The sides and the diagonals of the five regular solids are constructed by reference to the pentagon and the pentagram. Since in order to construct the pentagon and the pentagram it is necessary to cut a line in extreme and mean ratio, that is, the golden section ratio, and since all the regular solids flow from this step and are brought into unity by proportion within the sphere,[34] it can be said that "the golden section binds the five regular bodies in a rational way into a symphony ruled by an irrational proportion."[35]

Thus did Plato establish the primacy of order in the visible, tangible world. This order consists of ratio and proportion, primarily continuous geometrical proportions, but also including arithmetical proportions. Continuous geometrical proportions based on irrational ratios bind the world together, bind the matter of the world together, and even define the atomic plane surfaces of which primary bodies are composed. In order for a soul to know the visible, tangible world, it must be able to know measure and proportion based on two-dimensional arithmetical and three-dimensional geometrical proportions. Therefore, the creator god divided the soul of the world in accordance with these proportions, as we have seen. When the god created the immortal part of the human soul he also divided it according to these same proportions.[36] The human soul when first placed in a body is disordered and requires training and disciplining in order to be able to function properly. When properly trained in the sciences of arithmetic, plane geometry, and solid geometry, the human soul is able to form correct opinions and make correct judgment about the visible, tangible world.[37]

One aspect of the cosmos remains to be discussed. That is the sun, moon, planets, and fixed stars. Plato's creator god also brought order through measure and proportion to the functioning of these celestial bodies. First he placed these seven bodies in concentric circles at distances from the earth and each other corresponding to the combined double and triple continuous geometrical proportions, namely the series 1, 2, 3, 4, 8, 9, 27, which are the primary divisions of world soul and human souls. The creator god then set them in circular motions proportionally to each other. The god is herein establishing order in time, as he has established order in space with respect to the material world and matter of the world. The observable rotations of the sun and the other celestial bodies will, Plato says, teach men arithmetical units.[38]

To come to correct understanding about the movements of the celestial bodies, the human soul requires the training of astronomy, according to Plato.[39] With mastery of astronomy in addition to the previously prescribed arithmetic and plane and solid geometry, human beings can become capable of correct understanding of the visible, tangible world to the extent that is possible on the basis of knowing that world without knowing the pure forms of the intelligible world (which are the models for everything in the visible world). Plato believed that it is given to only a very few to know the forms of the intelligible world through the science of dialectic and thus to lay hold of real being with the unshakeable grasp of rational knowledge. Only such men, Plato says in the *Republic,* are fit to govern.[40]

The account is now complete, although in summary form of course, of Plato's case for the primacy of order in the unchanging word of real being and in the transitory world of becoming. From the present comparative evolutionary perspective on the formative process of social order, it appears that his account of the primacy and nature of order in the intelligible and visible worlds flows directly from his position that both the one and the many are real—which immediately required him to deal with the relationship between the one and the many. The account was so plausible, comprehensive, and fruitful that Plato became and remains the seminal figure in Western philosophy. Idealism in Western civilization begins with, and never escapes from, the eternal and universal nature that Plato gave to truth, beauty, and goodness.

Notes

1. Plato, *Theaetetus,* p. 152. Kirk and Raven say that Plato herein is inaccurate, that Heraclitus's position was that there is constant flux in the cosmos, but the stability that persists through it is of vital importance. G. S. Kirk and J. E. Raven, *The Presocratic Philosophers* (Cambridge: Cambridge Univ. Press, 1962), pp. 186–187.
2. Plato, *Theaetetus,* p. 157.
3. Sir Thomas L. Heath, ed. & trans., *The Thirteen Books of Euclid's Elements,* 2nd rev. ed. (Cambridge: Cambridge Univ. Press, 1926), 3: notes to Euclid X, 1, 15.
4. Plato, *Theaetetus,* p. 183.
5. Marcel Granet, *La Pensée Chinoise* (Paris: Michel, 1950), p. 273.
6. Ibid., p. 151 *et seq.*
7. The circle arises from the square, but by the intermediary of the hexagon. In a square with a side of 2 a demi-hexagon will have a base of 2 and three sides of 1. (The ratio of heaven to earth is 3 to 2, since the inaccuracy of making *pi* equal to 3 times the diameter of the circle is overlooked and the ratio is taken from the diameter of the circle which is also the side of the square earth and the circumference of the semicircle above, thus giving an odd *(yang)* number, 3, to superior Heaven, and an even *(yin)* number, 2, to inferior Earth). A right-angled triangle formed by dropping a perpendicular from the point of intersection of the side and the top of the demi-hexagon will have a hypotenuse twice the length of the side by the base. To figure the gnomon, the perpendicular is given the value of the emperor's height. If his height were 7 "feet" the incommensurable triangle 7, 4, 8+ was used with a multiplier of 9, i.e., 9 units to the "foot." Two "feet" were added. (The mythological reason for this is

that in ancient times the communication between Heaven and Earth was cut. This would appear, however, to explain why the order of Heaven was not *automatically* and perfectly realized in the Earth and therefore why it was necessary for good men, and the emperor preeminently, to assist in that realization. Practically, in the construction of the chariot—which represented the structure of Heaven and Earth—the added two feet provided clearance between the head and the curved roof.) Therefore, the gnomon was 9 × 7 (63) plus 2 × 9 (18) equals 81. If, on the other hand, the height of the emperor were 8 "feet," the incommensurable triangle 8, 4, 9 – was used with the multiplier 8, i.e., 8 units to the "foot." Then the gnomon was 8 × 8 (64) plus 2 × 8 (16) equals 80. As indicated the difference of one was ignored as the play of imperial and symbolic unity, so the dimensions were always the same. (The "feet" were woven mats which were laid end to end for measurement.) Granet, pp. 260–276.

8. Francis MacD. Cornford, trans., *Plato's Cosmology: The Timaeus of Plato* (New York, NY.: Bobbs-Merrill, n.d.), pp. 168–169.

9. Ibid., p. 173, fn. 1.

10. G. S. Kirk and J. E. Raven, *The Presocratic Philosphers* (Cambridge: Cambridge Univ. Press, 1962), pp. 418–419.

11. Cornford, p. 166.

12. Ibid., pp. 31–33.

13. Ibid., p. 34.

14. Ibid., pp. 39–40.

15. Plato, *Sophist,* p. 253.

16. Plato, *Timaeus,* p. 35.

17. Cornford, pp. 43–45. "Amity" is a reference to the Philia of Empedocles's system, which Kirk and Raven translate as "Love." Since Plato rules out the periodic destruction of the world, he does not refer to the contrary principle of Neikos in Empedocles's system, which Kirk and Raven translate as "Strife." Kirk and Raven, p. 327.

18. Sixty-four is also a square number (8^2). But this is of no significance for present purposes.

19. Matila Ghyka, "The Pythagorean and Platonic Scientific Criterion of the Beautiful in Classical Western Art," in F.S.C. Northrop, ed., *Ideological Differences and World Order* (Westport, CT: Greenwood Press, 1971), p. 95.

20. Ibid., p. 93.

21. Ibid.

22. Ibid.

23. Cornford, p. 66.

24. Ibid., pp. 66–72.

25. Ibid., p. 198.

26. Heath, 13: 18, 3: 508.

27. Ibid.

28. Cornford, p. 219.

29. Heath, notes to Euclid 4: 10, 2: 97–100.

30. Ghyka, pp. 94–98.

31. Ibid., pp. 92, 101, 110, 112–113.

32. Ibid., p. 113.

33. LeCorbusier (Charles E. Jeanneret-Gris), *The Modulor,* 2d ed., trans. Peter de Francia & Anna Bostock (Cambridge, MS.: M.I.T. Press, 1968), *passim;* Heath

Licklider, *Architectural Scale* (New York, NY.: George Braziller, 1965), pp. 30–59; Steen E. Rasmussen, *Experiencing Architecture* (Cambridge, MS.: M.I.T. Press, 1962), pp. 104–126.
34. Heath, Euclid 13.
35. This was said by Campanus of Novara in the Thirteenth century and quoted with approval by Pacioli in his 1509 treatise. Ghyka, pp. 98, 112.
36. Cornford, pp. 137 *et seq.*
37. Plato, *Timaeus,* pp. 42–44, *Republic,* 6–7: 504–534.
38. Cornford, pp. 72–136.
39. Plato, *Republic,* 7: 527–533, *Laws,* 8: 820–822, 12: 966–968.
40. Plato, *Republic,* 6–7: 504–534, *Laws,* 7: 817–822, 12: 966–968.

5

Universal Truth and Practical Wisdom

Plato's prescription for achieving the good society—that philosophers must rule—depends upon the utilization of knowledge of the highest truth for the solution of practical problems. Plato assumes the feasibility of such utilization in his famous allegory of the cave. Those few who have come up all the way from perception of shadows to full view of the sun and have grasped the highest truth will not be allowed to remain on the heights, but by "persuasion or constraint" will be induced to return to watch over and care for the other citizens. And it is specifically, though allegorically, asserted that because of their knowledge of the highest truth philosophers will have practical wisdom. Socrates says that the philosophers who are forced to return as kings shall be told:

> You must go down, then, each in his turn, to live with the rest and let your eyes grow accustomed to the darkness. You will then see a thousand times better than those who live there always; you will recognize every image for what it is and know what it represents, because you have seen justice, beauty, and goodness in their reality.[1]

However, when Plato turns from allegory to exposition, he fails to provide a methodology for translating highest truth into practical wisdom. His description of how the soul rises from the realm of sensed experience to highest truth is full and specific, but he disposes of the return journey in a short, cryptic passage.[2] Plato divides cognition into four hierarchically ordered stages, two for apprehending the visible world and two for the intelligible world. The lowest stage, imagining, grasps the images or shadows of material objects. The next, belief, grasps the material objects themselves. In the intelligible world, thinking, which employs assumptions and makes use of images, grasps mathematical objects such as atomic triangles and regular solids. And, finally, dialectic lays hold of pure forms or ideas. Training in mathematics enabled the soul to move up from imagining to belief to thinking and then to dialectic.[3] The Greeks distinguished between calculation and arithmetic, which was the theory of number.[4] Turning from calculation, or the counting of material objects, to the theory of number began the process of leading the soul towards pure ideas. Plane geometry, solid geometry, and astronomy continued the process. After ten years of training in mathematics in Plato's academy, the future philosophers received five years of training in dialectic.

Within the realm of forms, or pure ideas, there was also a hierarchy, leading to the highest truth, which was the pure form of the Good. Plato compared the Good in the intelligible world with the sun in the visible world. "[T]he Sun not only makes the things we see visible, but also brings them into existence and gives them growth and nourishment." Similarly, the objects of pure knowledge in the intelligible world "derive from the Good not only their power of being known, but their very being and reality."[5] Because the Good was above, and generated and nourished all the other forms in the realm of pure knowledge, Plato called it the "first principle."[6]

In the following passage Plato concludes his description of the four stages of cognition with an explanation of the dialectic by which the first principle of all knowledge is reached—and then he adds the few phrases that constitute his only statement about translating highest truth into practical wisdom:

> Then by the second section of the intelligible world you may understand me to mean all that unaided reasoning apprehends by the power of dialectic, when it treats its assumptions, not as first principles, but as *hypotheses* in the literal sense, things 'laid down' like a flight of steps up which it may mount all the way to something that is not hypothetical, the first principle of all; and having grasped this, may turn back and, holding on to the consequences which depend upon it, descend at last to a conclusion, never making use of any sensible object, but only of Forms, moving through Forms from one to another, and ending with Forms.[7]

Clearly the methodology that Plato offers does not support the claim of his allegory. The Guardians, having been taught to know the pure form or idea of the highest truth, are allegorically said to be a thousand times more capable than untrained persons of seeing things as they actually are in the world of sensed experience. They will "recognize every image for what it is and know what it represents." But the methodological statement indicates that, if the Philosopher who has grasped the pure form of highest knowledge returns into the world of sensed experience as Guardian, he can not take any implication of that knowledge with him because his reasoning ends in forms of the intelligible world and never enters into the visible world at all! The claim of infallible truth as the warrant to govern without a methodology to determine the implications of that truth for the direction and control of practical affairs may not have been the basis of Plato's own preference for totalitarian polity as Popper suggests, but it surely is the paradigmatic justification for regimes that purport to embody utopian goals but in fact serve the interests of those in power.[8]

Modern science makes the transition from highest truth back down into the world of sensed experience by deducing theorems from its hypothesized set of first principles and then devising experiments to test the theorems. The experimental method depends upon establishing epistemic correlates between the real world in which oxidization of fuel consists of the rapid movement of atoms and the sensed world in which a fire is seen as leaping tongues of yellow flame and felt as warmth. The logical implications of the set of hypothetical principles that constitute a theory in physics or chemistry are deduced. An experiment must then be devised to see whether the resulting theorems are true or false. If an implication of a set of principles is that under specified conditions a light wave of a given length will be produced, the experimenter must determine how to "see" whether that light wave is in fact produced when he creates the specified condition with his laboratory equipment. If the wave length lies within the spectrum of light visible to the human eye, he will need to determine the visible color that is the epistemic correlate of the light wave. The experimenter will need to station someone with normal color vision where the experimentally produced light wave will be visible. He then activates his equipment to produce the conditions which his theorem tells him should produce a light wave of the specified length. If the equipment works properly, the theorem is verified if the observer sees a specified color and falsified if he does not.[9]

The underlined phrases in the above quotation indicate that Plato had reached the first step in the experimental method. Having grasped the first principle of all, the dialectic turns back and holding onto the consequences of the first principle descends without the aid of any sensible object until it reaches a conclusion. This is the step, in modern science, of deducing the implications of the hypothetical premises. What Plato could not establish in any rigorous way was the correlation between his deduced conclusion (theorem) which was in the real world, and an object or event in the sensible world. Of course we need not fault him for this; no one else was able to solve this problem for the next two thousand years. Furthermore, the problem was more difficult for Plato. Modern science assumes that the real world is composed of material objects, such as atoms, molecules, cells, etc., which are in motion in relation to each other. Real material objects and their interactions are correlated with sensed material objects and their interactions. A light wave of a given length is correlated with an observed color, or an interaction between subatomic particles is correlated with a curved line on a photograph theoretically caused when a particle (which may have existed for less than one millionth of a second) plowed a tiny furrow through the photographic emulsion. But Plato had the problem of trying to correlate real, nonmaterial forms and their purely rational relationships with sensible material objects and their observed interactions. Moreover, even if Plato had been able to solve the problems of establishing correlates between entities and relationships in the real world and objects and interactions in the sensed world, he still would have had to struggle with the question of whether methods of systematic investigation that are appropriate for knowing and predicting in the physical and biological worlds are equally appropriate for knowing and prescribing in the realm of the cultural processes by which human societies are formed and human interactions are regulated. In any event Plato, although overwhelmingly persuasive on the point that the world is characterized by—indeed held together by—a rational order, was unable to provide a rigorous, objective method for determining the implications of that rational order for the organization of society and the regulation of human affairs.

Aristotle developed a theory in which universals are closer to particulars. Aristotelian universals do not have a real existence outside and apart from particulars, but exist first in sensed particulars and then are grasped by logical abstraction. Aristotle's logical classifications, upon which the biological sciences are based, are not as completely abstract as Plato's mathematical ratios. "The species take account of the specific character, and the genera of the generic character."[10] "Classification," Whitehead says, "is a halfway house between the immediate concreteness of the individual thing and the complete abstraction of mathematic notions," and modern physical science depends upon complete, mathematical abstractions.[11] "The popularity of Aristotelian Logic retarded the advance of physical science throughout the Middle Ages."[12]

It was not Aristotle, however, but the Stoics who first developed a widely accepted and immensely influential methodology for determining the implications for human affairs of rational order in the universe. Zeno of Citium, the founder of Stoicism, lived from 336 to 264 B.C. and began to teach in Athens around 300 B.C. The previous three-hundred-year effort of Greek natural philosophers to synthesize accumulated human experience in a systematic, noncontradictory set of objective, persistent, universal concepts had apparently resulted in general acceptance among the learned men of Greece of the view that the universe is characterized by a rational order. In any event, the Stoics did not find it necessary to give much attention to proving the existence and nature of rational order; they assumed its existence and accepted an amalgamated Platonic-Aristotelian account of its nature. The unique contribution of the Stoics was a social ethic.

By a social ethic I mean a set of objectively valid specifications of right and wrong behavior, derived by accepted canons of reasoning from agreed implications of the highest truth. Not that the Stoics solved the problem that Plato failed to solve. They did not find a way to move by rigorous steps from the highest truth to practical wisdom. But they did develop a way of moving by rigorous steps from certain *agreed implications of the highest truth* to practical wisdom. For Plato the highest truth and the highest good were identical. The Stoics maintained this identification, but from the perspective of the knower—it is good to know the rational order of the universe and to act accordingly. The Stoics held that all persons (of maturity and sound mind) are capable of knowing the rational order of the universe and therefore should be charged with the moral responsibility of knowing it correctly and of acting accordingly.[13]

The Stoics took very seriously the acquisition of the least bit of knowledge. The path to truth began with a flash of light or a brief sound which consisted of radiating waves which were met by mind waves. The result was a "sensation," or "mind-picture." At this early point in the acquisition of knowledge the Stoic was called upon to exercise the patience, care, perseverance, and objectivity that we expect of the modern experimental scientist. The observer's mind received a flash of light, or sound, but Stoicism placed the observer under the obligation to determine whether the mind was grasping something real and true or recording an illusion or phantasm. The observer was admonished to approach this decision with the intention of mastering the object, to give careful attention, to guard against undue haste or feebleness of will, and to make sure that the picture had the "clearness" that attaches to a real object but not to a phantasm. The observer then was to decide whether to assent to the received mind-picture as a true mind-picture, to negate it as false, to remain quiescent regarding the matter, or to suspend judgment. Assent wrongly given led to "opinion" instead of truth. The seriousness with which the Stoics viewed this early step in the path to truth is indicated by the fact that wrong assent was held to be error and sin.[14]

Following assent to the mind-picture, the Stoic truth-seeker "ratified" the assent given by grasping the image of a particular external object and fixing it irrevocably in the mind, where it became a "comprehension-picture" and a unit of knowledge. In modern usage it would be called a perception. The memory retained perceptions and the mind compared them through various modes of reasoning, such as "similitude," "analogy," "transference," and "opposition." From perceptions plus such reasoning arose "notions" or "rational mind-pictures," which we would call conceptions. A class concept, such as table—as distinguished from this table or that table—would be a rational mind-picture. As with mind-pictures, so with rational mind-pictures, the Stoic truth-seeker was admonished to seriously and carefully investigate and then assent to the true and reject the false. True rational mind-pictures, or true conceptions, were available for further combinations into higher conceptions. Another element in the Stoic system of knowledge was "common notions," or common conceptions. All perceptions, all conceptions, and all common conceptions were then combined into one all-embracing, internally consistent system of knowledge. This final step in the pursuit of truth the Stoics called "science."[15]

It was the particular genius of the Roman Stoic philosophers and jurisconsults to apply this theory of knowledge to human interactions of daily life. In the course of applying it to human affairs the Roman Stoics added a prescriptive element to the system of knowledge. The result was a hierarchically ordered system of perceptions, conceptions, common conceptions, and prescriptions, the whole of which was believed to constitute the objective, universal order of human activities and of the universe in which those activities occurred. The obligation which the prescriptions carried did not arise from human will or reason. Human beings were obligated to act in accordance with the prescriptions because reason had discovered that such actions were in accordance with human nature and contrary actions would be against it.[16]

Reading the discussions of the Roman jurisconsults in the light of the Stoic theory of knowledge it appears that common conceptions were metaphysical postulates and their logical implications. The metaphysical postulates included: (1) There is a rational order in the universe; (2) Human beings possess reason and therefore can know the rational order of the universe. A logical implication would be that the same effect will always follow from the same cause. These metaphysical postulates and their logical implications would provide conceptions such as "person," "cause," and "effect." Assuming this to be the meaning of the Stoic "common" conceptions, they will be called "postulational conceptions" in order clearly to distinguish them, by origin, from conceptions derived from observation of human activity, which will be called "perceptual conceptions." An examination of the way in which the Roman jurisconsults developed the conception of "negligence," in the Lex Aquilia, shows the interrelationships between postulational conceptions, perceptions, perceptual conceptions, and prescriptions.

If the Roman Stoic philosophers and jurisconsults had validated rules of law solely by reference to the practice of the community with respect to that kind of activity, they would have accomplished nothing more than to give formal structure to the dependence upon custom that is familiar in traditional societies. If they had, on the other hand, validated rules of law solely by deductive reasoning from metaphysical postulates, Roman private law would not have had the evident pertinence for the regulation of human interactions that led the whole of the modern world to accept and use Roman categories of juristic thought. What the Roman Stoic philosophers and jurisconsults did was to validate rules of law by reference to the whole system of knowledge, which included both postulational and perceptual conceptions. This did not create a one-to-one relationship of a law with a given set of activities such as training apprentices, or transporting cargo, or treating the sick, to rules of law governing, respectively, each of those activities. Instead the Romans sought out the common element in many such sets of activities and formulated the common element into a high-level conception.[17] However, in order to discern a common element it was necessary to bring to the process of observing human activities the implications of postulational conceptions.

For example, "negligence" in the Lex Aquilia generalized observed community experience in a number of seemingly quite diverse sets of activities, including the following: a shoemaker correcting his apprentice; a porter throwing off a load that was too heavy for him; a physician administering a drug to a sick person; a surgeon undertaking an operation; a boisterous young man throwing another into a river; a driver of a wagon pulled by a team of mules; young men practicing javelin throwing; and a barber shaving a customer.[18] The common element in these (and other) activities was the likelihood of injury to others under certain conditions. The apprentice had lost sight in one eye when the shoemaker struck him in the back of the neck with a heavy last. A bystander was killed when the porter could not safely set down his too-heavy load. The patient died when the physician administered a potion that a competent physician would have known to be poisonous. The surgeon undertook an operation beyond his skill. The river into which the young man was thrown was so swift that no one could survive in it. The driver did not have the strength to control the mule team and a bystander was crushed against a building by the wagon. The javelin throwers were practicing close to a field where slaves were working and a javelin killed a slave. The barber was shaving a customer outdoors near a ball game and the ball hit his hand driving the razor into the customer's throat.[19]

It was necessary to make use of the postulational conception that events have rational causes in order to identify likelihood of injury to others as a common element in these disparate activities. In light of the postulational conception of causation, physical injuries are seen to be the effect of causes in the forces and agencies of tools, vehicles, substances, and the acts of animals and human beings. (According to the belief that previously had prevailed in the Mediterranean area the gods pushed and pulled things about and were responsible for the outcome of events.)

Another common element in all the activities enumerated above was seen to be that in every case the likelihood of injury to others was foreseeable. This is implied by the postulational conceptions that the same effect will always follow from the same cause, and that human beings can know causes and their effects. From the common elements of likelihood of injury, and foreseeability of that likelihood, the Roman jurisconsults constructed the legal conception of "negligence." Negligence was action which was, or could have been, known, under the circumstances, to be likely to injure another.

What does fidelity to human nature require of persons who are in situations in which it is foreseeable that contemplated action, under the circumstances, is likely to result in injury to others? The three precepts of the Roman law were to live honestly, not to injure another, and to give to another that which was his. These obligations were deemed to be appropriate in a society of rational human beings. A person who was capable of knowing the causes of effects and who was capable of some control over those causes was obligated by self-respect and decent regard for peers to refrain from setting in train causes which were likely to result in injury to others. Not to refrain was to be responsible for the injury—as much so when the causal acts were done in negligent disregard of the likelihood of injury as when the causal acts were done with the intention of producing the injurious effects. Accordingly, the Lex Aquilia prescribed that every person is liable for injuries caused by his negligence.

If a resident of Roma, Carthago, Lutetia (Paris), Londinium, Alexandria, Tarsus, Rhodus, or Athenae were to ask, Why should I obey the Lex Aquilia? the appropriate answer was, In truth, you must! To obey was to act in accordance with human nature and the nature of the universe as understood by right reason.[20] Truth was a comprehensive system composed of perceptions, perceptual conceptions, postulational conceptions, legal conceptions, and prescriptions. And the whole system was the warrant for requiring compliance with any of the prescriptions. If rights and duties, benefits and burdens were distributed in accordance with the objective system of truth, the social order was just. Truth was the ultimate standard for distributive justice. Truth was also the warrant for requiring the actions and restraints that were necessary to establish and maintain a just social order. Not to accept such a social order, not to obey the rules of such a legal system, was to deny that the stars run in their courses, that the same effect follows the same cause, that human beings are rational. Cicero put it this way:

> True law is right reason in agreement with nature; it is of universal application, unchanging and everlasting; it summons to duty by its commands, and averts from wrongdoing by its prohibition. And it does not lay its commands or prohibitions upon good men in vain, though neither have any effect on the wicked. It is a sin to try to alter this law nor is it allowable to attempt to repeal any part of it, and it is impossible to abolish it entirely. We cannot be freed from its obligations by senate or people, and we need not look outside ourselves for an expounder or interpreter of it. And there will not be different laws at Rome and at Athens, or different laws now and in the future, but one eternal and unchangeable law will be valid for all nations and all times, and there will be one master and ruler, that is, God, over us all, for he is the author of this law, its promulgator, and its enforcing judge. Whoever is disobedient is fleeing from himself and denying his human nature, and by reason of this very fact he will suffer the worst penalties, even if he escapes what is commonly considered punishment.[21]

Notes

1. Francis MacD. Cornford, trans., *The Republic of Plato* (London: Oxford Univ. Press, 1976), p. 234.
2. Ibid., pp. 223–226.
3. Ibid., pp. 227, 235–250.
4. Ibid., p. 240.
5. Ibid., p. 220.
6. Ibid., pp. 225.
7. Ibid. (Emphasis added).
8. K. R. Popper, *The Open Society and Its Enemies* (Princeton, NJ: Princeton Univ. Press, 1963), vol. 1.
9. F. S. C. Northrop, *The Logic of the Sciences and the Humanities* (New York, NY: Macmillan, 1947), pp. 119–123.
10. Alfred N. Whitehead, "Mathematics as an Element in the History of Thought," in *The World of Mathematics*, ed. Newman (New York, NY: Simon & Schuster, 1956), 1: 409.
11. Ibid.
12. Ibid.
13. E. Vernon Arnold, *Roman Stoicism* (London: Routledge & Kegan Paul, 1958), pp. 143–144, 213–214.
14. Ibid., pp. 130–132.
15. Ibid., pp. 133–141. See also F. H. Sandbach, *The Stoics* (New York, NY.: W. W. Norton, 1975), pp. 85–94; J. M. Rist, *Stoic Philosophy* (Cambridge: Univ. Press, 1969), pp. 133–151.
16. Arnold, pp. 72, 128–129.
17. Rudolph Sohm, *The Institutes* 3rd. ed., (South Hackensack, NJ: Rothman Reprints, 1970), pp. 30–33.
18. Samuel P. Scott, *The Civil Law* (Cincinnati: The Central Trust Co., 1932), 3: 323–327.

19. Ibid.
20. Arnold, pp. 281–284.
21. Cicero, *The Republic*, trans. Clinton W. Keyes (Cambridge, MA: Harvard Univ. Press, 1948), p. 211.

6

Changes in Roman Society and Law

The legal conception of negligence in the Lex Aquilia depends upon reasoning from observed events by means of perceptions and perceptual conceptions; but it also depends upon reasoning from metaphysical postulates by means of postulational conceptions. The significance of the latter component can be seen by comparing the conception of negligence in the Lex Aquilia with the conception of neglect in Section 245 of the Babylonian Laws of Hammu-Rabi: "If a man has hired an ox and causes its death by neglect or by striking (it), he shall replace ox by ox to the owner of the ox."[1]

It is often said that the Roman law has a logical structure, whereas earlier law codes consisted of a mere collection of legal rules. For instance, the provisions of Hammu-Rabi's code concerning oxen are:[2]

Section 241. If a man takes an ox as a distress, he shall pay ⅓ maneh of silver.

Sections 242-3. If a man has hired (oxen) for 1 year, he shall give 4 GUR of corn (as) the hire of a rear ox, (and) 3 GUR of corn (as) the hire of a fore-ox to its owner.

Sections 244-5. If a man has hired an ox (or) an ass and a lion kills it in the open country, it is the owner's (risk).

[as above.]

Section 246. If a man has hired an ox and breaks its leg or cuts the sinew of its neck, he shall replace ox by ox to the owner of the ox.

Section 247. If a man has hired an ox and puts out its eye, he shall give half its price (in) silver to the owner of the ox.

Section 248. If a man has hired an ox and has broken its horn, injures its tail or gashes (?) its shoulder (?) he shall give (him) a fifth of its price (in) silver.

Section 249. If a man has hired an ox and a god has struck it and it dies, the man who has hired the ox may take an oath by the life of a god and he then goes free.

Section 250. If an ox as it passes along a street has gored a man and causes his death, that case affords no cause of action.

Section 251. If the man's ox is wont to gore and his district has notified him that (it is) wont to gore and he has not screened its horn (or) has not tied (it) up and that ox has gored the son of a (free) man and so has caused (his) death, he shall give ½ maneh of silver.

Section 252. If (the victim is) the slave of a (free) man, he shall give ⅓ maneh of silver.

D. G. Lyon, writing in the *Journal of the American Oriental Society,* argued that Hammu-Rabi's code did, indeed, have a logical structure, and that the quoted provisions concerning oxen exemplified that structure. He pointed out that the provisions on oxen were grouped together with laws concerning farming and, Lyon said, the ox was the principal farm animal of the Babylonians.[3] What Lyon succeeded in showing was that Hammu-Rabi's code had the logical structure of a prescriptive order based solely upon perceptual conceptions. Laws on seizing oxen for debt, annual rates of hire for oxen, and liability for injury done to oxen and done by oxen are grouped together on the basis of observations of the role of oxen in a Babylonian community. The juxtaposition of the legal provisions is determined by experience accumulated in perceptions and perceptual conceptions.

The structure of classical Roman private law can best be seen in Justinian's Institutes, which are a clear and simple statement of Roman law. Title I of Book I of the Institutes is headed "Concerning Justice and Law," and begins with the sentence: "Justice is the constant and perpetual desire to give to each one that to which he is entitled." The immediately following paragraphs are:

(1) Jurisprudence is the knowledge of matters divine and human, and the comprehension of what is just and unjust.

(2) [The laws will be explained simply first, in the Institutes, and then in full, in the Code and the Digest.]

(3) The following are the precepts of the Law: to live honestly, not to injure another, and to give to each one that which belongs to him.

(4) There are two branches of this study, namely: public and private. Public Law is that which concerns the administration of the Roman government; Private Law relates to the interests of individuals.[4]

Only a few sentences are devoted to public law; all the rest of the Institutes concern private law. The main headings show the basic structure of Roman private law. They are: definition of a legal person; types of relations between legal persons; division and classification of things; definition and classification of relations of persons to things; transmission of rights with respect to things from one person to another; obligations arising from contract; obligations arising from delictual actions; legal actions for the correction of injustices.

It will be apparent that the legal provisions concerning oxen, which are grouped together in Hammu-Rabi's code, would be distributed among several categories in Roman law: Seizure of oxen for debt would appear under legal actions; annual rates of hire, under obligations arising from contract; liability for injury done to oxen and by oxen, under obligations arising from delictual actions.

The new structure first appeared in the eighteen volumes which earned the Roman Stoic Q. Mucius Scaevola recognition as the founder of Roman private law.[5] According to Sohm, the great German historian of Roman law, Scaevola "was the first to determine, in clear outline, the nature of legal institutions (will, legacy, guardianship, partnership, sale, hiring, etc.) and their various kinds (genera)."[6] For the first time there was a juristic science. Sohm states the significance of such a science:

> A scientific exposition, for example, would never run as follows: If a thing has been delivered to you under a contract of sale, you have the right to keep it, and a third party into whose possession it comes is bound to hand it over to you. [This statement tracks the steps in an observed transaction known by perceptual conceptions.] The scientific exposition would be in this fashion. First, ownership is a right, unlimited in its contents, to exercise control over a thing. Thus we get the conception of ownership. Secondly, ownership can be acquired by traditio, occupatio, usucaptio, & c. (each of these terms being defined). Thus in place of a series of legal rules we have a number of abstract conceptions, partly of rights, partly of facts.[7]

Not only would the several provisions on oxen not be grouped together in Roman law, but also no provision of law would be self-sufficient. In the case of Hammu-Rabi's proscription of neglect of an ox, on the other hand, that provision, in itself, would be sufficient to enable the Babylonian judge to apply it in particular cases. The Babylonian judge would understand every term in Section 245 by reference to a world known by perceptual conceptions. "Man" would be understood to be an instance of a class concept derived from perceptions of creatures of human appearance and male characteristics going about their daily activities in a Babylonian farming community. "Hiring an ox" would be understood in terms of the observed experience in a Babylonian community of paying money for the temporary use of the principal farm animal. "Causing its death" and "neglect" would also be understood by reference to the observed experience of a Babylonian farm community accumulated in perceptions and perceptual conceptions. Every term in the Babylonian law would be understood by reference to observed experience of the Babylonian community.

In the case of applying the Lex Aquilia to a case in which the death of a hired ox is alleged to have been caused by negligence, the law can not be understood by reference to the experience of the community in which it occurred. The necessity of referring to postulational conceptions in order to understand "negligence" has been demonstrated above. Even more important is the matter of correctly understanding the legal conception of the person who is alleged to have been negligent. The referent of the term used to indicate the legal person (such as "one who" or "if a person") is not an instance of a class concept derived from perceptions of creatures of human appearance and male characteristics going about their daily activities in an experienced community. The nature of a legal person is determined by reference to the first division of Roman private law, namely, definition of legal persons.

The conception of a legal person in Roman private law is derived from the metaphysical postulate that human beings possess reason which enables them to know the postulated rational order of the universe, and from the postulational conception that human beings have the moral obligation to know their true nature and to live accordingly. According to Roman Stoicism, to "know thyself" was to recognize that one's inner nature is an image of the rational order of the universe. Cicero says:[8]

> . . . but out of all the material of the philosophers' discussions, surely there comes nothing more valuable than the full realization that we are born for Justice, and that right is based, not upon men's opinions, but upon Nature. This fact will immediately be plain if you once get a clear conception of man's fellowship and union with his fellow-men. For no single thing is so like another, so exactly its counterpart, as all of us are to one another.

There was abundant opportunity for the postulational conceptions of Roman Stoic philosophy to find their way into the legal conceptions of classical Roman private law. Of the fourteen persons who are generally credited with developing the Roman juristic science during the republic, eleven are known to have been Stoics or heavily influenced by Stoicism.[9] In the first century of the principate Stoicism was becoming the recognized creed of the great majority of educated persons in Rome and, in the time of emperors Antoninus Pius and Marcus Aurelius, Stoicism inspired the full flowering of classical Roman private law.[10]

The legal person in classical Roman private law is an abstract conception derived by deductive reasoning from a metaphysical postulate and postulational conceptions. Therefore, the conception of a legal person in Roman law possesses the characteristics which Parmenides was so influential in imparting to the conceptions of reality in Western civilization, namely, noncontradiction, persistence, objectivity, and universality. The Roman legal person was not perceived in farming activities; was not perceived as male or female; was not perceived as having been born in a certain village; nor as worshipping at a particular hearth. Nothing of experience goes into the definition of the Roman legal person. The Roman legal person is postulated to be possessed of reason.

Experience does figure, however, in the determination of whether a particular perceived human being has legal personality. We learn from the division of the Roman law on definition of legal persons that certain factual events can negate the legal personality arising from postulation. Therefore, the Roman law on legal personality is concerned with slavery, minority, and guardianship. Nonpayment of debt, chronological immaturity, and demonstrated inability to manage one's affairs result in the affected persons being denied legal personality. (Only partially in the case of slavery under later Roman law.) However legal personality is by nature, loss of it is factual, and the occurrence of other facts may repair the loss. Payment of debt, reaching chronological maturity, or demonstrating capacity to manage one's affairs can remove the legal disabilities of slavery, minority, and guardianship.

It having been determined in a case under the Lex Aquilia that the parties had legal personality, reference would then have to be made seriatim to the divisions of law on classification of things, classifications of relations of persons to things, transmission of such rights; obligations arising from contract, and obligations arising from delictual actions. In each case the nature of the legal conception would have to be determined by reference to the logically related postulational conceptions derived by Artistotelean logic from the metaphysical postulates about the world we live in and human nature, and then it would have to be determined whether the factual events in the instant case fall within the abstract legal conceptions. That is, it would have to be determined whether oxen can be owned and possessed and whether this ox was owned by one of the parties and possessed by the other; whether legal rights in oxen can be transferred; whether these parties transferred a right of possession (including determination of the legal conception of a contract and whether the factual events in the present instance gave rise to a contract); the standard of due care that a lessee of an ox owes its owner, and whether that standard was met or breached; and the amount of injury. "Thus," as Sohm said, "in place of a series of legal rules we have a number of abstract conceptions, partly of rights [postulational conceptions], and partly of facts [perceptual conceptions].[11]

These developments in Roman private law reflect a change in fundamental beliefs. Events are now believed to occur because of a knowable cause, not because of the action of some god. In such a world those who can make wise decisions are those that can know causes and effects in a rationally ordered universe and can know the prescriptive order which will enable human beings to live in accordance with their true nature. The first impact in Rome of Stoic ideas was among intellectuals in the Scipionic circle in whose mouths Cicero places the dialogue of his *De Re Publica*. This was about thirty years before the Stoic Q. Mucius Scaevola wrote the volumes that began the restructuring of Roman law. The resulting juristic science was completely independent of previously existing Roman law and custom.[12] As the ideas of Stoic philosophy became generally prevailing beliefs, self-interested claims justified by the new beliefs resulted in changes in Roman society and law. The constitutional historian C. H. McIlwain said of these changes "There is probably no other social revolution in recorded history so important, so complete, so continuous over so long a period."[13]

The new beliefs carried a number of implications: that "property" was a bundle of rights of an individual to own, possess, use, and dispose of physical resources, instead of land belonging irrevocably to a family viewed as the continuity of paterfamiliases; that the holder of property rights could transfer those rights by will or inter vivos to others; that members of the next generation inherited the property rights, not an active personality deemed to be capable of approaching the gods efficaciously; that property rights indicated the persons who were recognized as having the authority to make decisions with respect to property to the extent of the right; that those who can know causes and effects in a rational world can make wise decisions, and all persons everywhere are equal in that capacity (except for factual disabilities) because all are, by nature, rational.

As these implications of Stoic beliefs became apparent, it was to be expected that daughters and younger sons would begin to claim shares in their father's property; that women would claim the right to own and manage property in their own name; and that daughters and younger sons would want to be emancipated from the control of father or eldest brother as paterfamilias; and that provincials throughout the Roman empire would claim the benefits and protection of Roman private law. These claims were often met voluntarily before changes had occurred in Roman law. Stoicism was widely taught in the homes of educated Romans as instruction for children and as a body of ethics.[14] All of these claims were recognized and given official status by changes made in Roman private law in the classical period.[15]

These implementations of Roman Stoic fundamental beliefs established basic principles and institutions of property law, family law, inheritance, and legal personality which are in use today in every country which inherited Western civilization. The earlier discussion of the derivation of the conception of negligence in the Lex Aquilia can now be seen as a part of the process of developing the basic principles and institution of tort law. Every person is deemed capable of knowing causes and effects in a rational world and capable of controlling his/her own acts in accordance with the precept not to injure another. Therefore every person will be held liable for injury to another caused by intentional or negligent acts.

Similarly, the Romans developed the basic principles and institutions of contract law. Because every person is equally capable of knowing causes and effects, everyone is deemed equally capable of anticipating the advantages and disadvantages of proposed courses of conduct and equally competent to decide what risks are involved in contingencies. Therefore, it is in the public interest that the courts should enforce obligations that each party is reasonably understood to have undertaken. Involved in this development is a whole new basis of legal obligation. In the earlier law of Rome (and other city-states), binding obligation arose from the sacred formula invoking the authority of the gods. This was formalistic. If the parties used the wrong words the legal obligation did not come into being. For instance in a case of wrongful cutting of vines, the aggrieved party recited the formula for establishing liability but he said "vines" whereas the formula said "trees" and it was held that obligation to compensate had not arisen.[16] In Roman private law, however, obligation arises from expression of the will of a rational/moral being, such as manifesting an intention to be bound, as in contract, or consciously doing a wrongful act, as in tort. This was entirely appropriate in a world in which it was believed that every human being, by nature, was capable of knowing the consequences of actions and was responsible for acting justly.

The characteristics of noncontradiction, persistence, universality, and objectivity in the conception of legal personality, and the creation of the formless juristic acts appropriate to such rational/moral persons, changed Roman law from the local law of a city-state to the universal law of a worldwide empire. (The latter is referred to herein as classical Roman private law.) The Greek city-states had fought themselves to exhaustion because they could not conceive of and implement a regime of law that would enable them to peacefully participate in the opportunities of trade throughout the Mediterranean world. As Rome conquered that world, national jealousies no longer stood in the way of peaceful intercourse, but it was still necessary to overcome the implication of the older beliefs that gods controlled events, that the domain of gods was limited to a single city-state, and that the gods were the only source of law. The implication was that those who did not have gods in common could not have law in common. The consequence was that foreign trade was hard to distinguish from raid and pillage.

Rome first dealt with this problem by entering into commercial treaties with other city-states under which citizens of Carthage, for instance, while in Rome, were subject to Roman law regarding commercial transactions, and vice versa. As Rome conquered more and more of the known world this practice became unsatisfactory. Numerous communities were annihilated. No local government existed which could enter into a commercial treaty with Rome, and yet the members of that community did not acquire Roman citizenship, except by special favor. All of the transactions of these nonprivileged aliens were not legally binding.

The recognition of formless juristic acts by persons deemed to be rational and moral by nature enabled the magistrate to bring the transactions of all persons everywhere in the known world under the regime of the new universal law that was emerging from social and legal implementation of the implications of the Roman Stoic beliefs about the world and human nature. The general acceptance of the fundamental beliefs of Roman Stoicism, towards the end of the republic, "marks the commencement of the process by which the local law of the city of Rome was gradually converted into what Roman law was destined at a future time to be, namely a general law for the civilized world."[17]

Notes

1. G. L. Driver & John C. Miles, eds., *The Babylonians* (Oxford: Clarendon Press, 1955), p. 87.
2. Ibid., pp. 87–89.
3. D. G. Lyon, "The Structure of the Hammu-Rabi Code," in *Journal of American Oriental Society,* 25:248, 1904.
4. Samuel P. Scott, *The Civil Law* (Cincinnati: The Central Trust Co., 1932), 2:5.
5. Rudolph Sohm, *The Institutes,* 3rd. ed. (South Hackensack, NJ: Rothman Reprints, 1970), 90–91. The time was about 100 B.C.
6. Ibid.
7. Ibid., pp. 32–33.
8. Cicero, *The Laws,* trans. Clinton W. Keyes (Cambridge, MS: Harvard Univ. Press, 1948), p. 329.
9. Herbert Jolowicz, *Historical Introduction to the Study of Roman Law* (Cambridge: Cambridge Univ. Press, 1939), pp. 90–91; E. Vernon Arnold, *Roman Stoicism* (London: Routledge & Kegan Paul, 1958), Ch. 5.
10. Arnold, Ch. 16.

11. See above.
12. Eugen Ehrlich, *Fundamental Principles of the Sociology of Law,* trans. Moll (Cambridge, MS: Harvard Univ. Press, 1936), pp. 260–261.
13. Charles H. McIlwain, *Constitutionalism, Ancient and Modern* (Ithaca, NY: Cornell Univ. Press, 1940), p. 54.
14. Arnold, Chs. 12–15.
15. Sohm, Secs. 11, 30, 32, 34, 61, 91, 108.
16. Numa Denis Fustel de Coulanges, *The Ancient City,* trans. Willard Small (Garden City, NY: Doubleday & Co., 1956), pp. 191–192.
17. Sohm, pp. 67–69.

Bibliography

Alexander, Lyle Thomas. "Chemical Properties of Soil," sec. 5 of "Soil." *Encyclopaedia Britannica*, vol. 20. Expo 70 ed. Chicago: Encyclopaedia Britannica, Inc., 1970. pp. 837–840.

Aristotle. *The Works of Aristotle*. Translated under the editorship of W. D. Ross. Oxford: Clarendon Press, 1908–1931.

Arnold, E. Vernon. *Roman Stoicism*. London: Routledge & Kegan Paul Ltd., 1958 (1911).

Bachofen, Johann Jakob. *Myth, Religion, and Mother Right: Selected Writings of J. J. Bachofen*. Trans. Ralph Manheim. Princeton, New Jersey: Princeton University Press, 1967.

Beattie, James Alexander. "Water." *Encyclopaedia Britannica*, vol. 23. Expo 70 ed. Chicago: Encyclopaedia Britannica, Inc., 1970. pp. 270–271.

Borchardt, Knut. "The Industrial Revolution in Germany, 1700–1914." Trans. George Hammersley. Chapter 4 in *The Fontana Economic History of Europe: vol. 4: 1700–1914, The Emergence of Industrial Societies*. Ed. Carlo M. Cipolla. London: Collins, 1972.

Chatterjee, S. and D. M. Datta. *An Introduction to Indian Philosophy*, 5th ed. Calcutta: University of Calcutta, 1954.

Cicero. *De Legibus*. Cambridge: Harvard University Press, 1948.

Cicero, Marcus, T. *The Republic*. Trans. Clinton Walker Keyes. Cambridge, MA: Harvard University Press, 1948.

Conti, Flavio. "Chapel at Ronchamp, France," in *The Grand Tour: Individual Creations*. Boston: HBJ Press, 1978. pp. 121–136.

Cornford, Francis MacDonald. Trans. com. *Plato's Cosmology: The Timaeus of Plato*. New York: Bobbs-Merrill Company, Inc., n.d.

Cornford, Francis MacDonald. Trans. with introduction and notes, *The Republic of Plato*. London: Oxford University Press, 1976 (1941).

Driver, G. L. and Miles, John C., eds. *The Babylonians*. Oxford: Clarendon Press, 1955.

Ehrlich, Eugen. *Fundamental Principles of the Sociology of Law*. Trans. Moll. Cambridge: Harvard University Press, 1936.

Elbe, Guenther von. "Combustion." *Encyclopaedia Britannica*, vol. 6. Expo 70 ed. Chicago: Encyclopaedia Britannica, Inc., 1970. pp. 126–128.

Euclid. *Elements* see Heath.

Freeman, Kathleen. *Greek City States*. New York: W. W. Norton & Company, Inc., 1950.

Fustel de Coulanges, Numa Denis. *The Ancient City: A Study on the Religion, Laws, and Institutions of Greece and Rome*. Trans. Willard Small. Garden City, New York: Doubleday and Company, Inc., 1956.

Ghyka, Matila. "The Pythagorean and Platonic Scientific Criterion of the Beautiful in Classical Western Art" in *Ideological Differences and World Order: Studies in the Philosophy and Science of the World's Cultures*. Ed. F.S.C. Northrop. Westport, CT: Greenwood Press, Pub., 1949, 1971. pp. 90–116.

Granet, Marcel. *La Pensee Chinoise*. Paris: A. Michel, 1950.

Greenidge, Abel Hendy Jones. *A Handbook of Greek Constitutional History*. London: Macmillan and Company, Ltd., 1896.

Guthrie, W. K. C. *The Greek Philosophers: From Thales to Aristotle*. New York: Harper and Row, 1960.

Harrison, A. R. W. *The Laws of Athens: The Family and Property* 1. Oxford: Clarendon Press, 1968.

Heath, Sir Thomas Little, ed., trans. *The Thirteen Books of Euclid's Elements,* 3 volumes. 2nd ed., rev. with additions. Cambridge: Cambridge University Press, 1926.

Holton, Gerald. "The Mainsprings of Discovery" in *The Nature of Scientific Discovery*. Ed. Owen Gingerich. Washington D.C.: Smithsonian Institution Press, 1975.

Holton, Gerald. "The Thematic Imagination in Science" in *Science and Culture: A Study of Cohesive and Disjunctive Forces*. Ed. Gerald Holton. Boston: Houghton Mifflin Company, 1965. pp. 88–108.

Holton, Gerald. *Thematic Origins of Scientific Thought*. Cambridge, Mass.: Harvard University Press, 1973.

Huxley, Julian. *Evolution, The Modern Synthesis*. New York and London: Harper & Brothers, 1943.

Jaspers, Karl. *The Origin and Goal of History*. Trans. Michael Bullock. New Haven: Yale University Press, 1953.

Jolowicz, Herbert. *Historical Introduction to the Study of Roman Law*. Cambridge: Cambridge University Press, 1939.

Kirk, G. S. and Raven, J. E. *The Presocratic Philosophers: A Critical History with a Selection of Texts*. Cambridge: Cambridge University Press, 1962.

Kramrisch, Stella. "Natural Science and Technology in Relation to Cultural Patterns and Social Practices in India," in *Philosophy and Culture-*

East and West. Ed. C. A. Moore. Honolulu: University of Hawaii Press, 1961. pp. 156–171.

Le Corbusier (Jeanneret-Gris, Charles Edouard). *The Modulor,* 2nd ed. Trans. Peter de Francia and Anna Bostock. Cambridge, MA: M.I.T. Press, 1968.

Levy-Bruhl, Lucien. *How Natives Think*. Trans. Lilian A. Clare. New York: A Knopf, 1926.

Licklikder, Heath. *Architectural Scale*. New York: George Braziller, Inc., 1965.

Lyon, D. G. "The Structure of the Hammu-Rabi Code." *Journal of American Oriental Society* 25 (1904):248.

McIlwain, Charles H. *Constitutionalism, Ancient and Modern*. Ithaca: Cornell University Press, 1940.

Monod, Jacques. *Chance and Necessity*. Trans. A. Wainhouse. New York: Alfred A. Knopf, 1971.

Munitz, Milton K. "Cosmology" in vol. 2 of *Encyclopaedia of Philosophy*. Ed. Paul Edwards. New York: Macmillan Pub. Company, Inc. and The Free Press, 1967. pp. 237–244.

Northrop, F. S. C. *The Logic of the Sciences and the Humanities*. New York: Macmillan Company, 1947.

Northrop, F. S. C. *The Meeting of East and West: An Inquiry Concerning World Understanding*. New York: Macmillan Company, 1946.

Northrop, F. S. C. *Science and First Principles*. New York: Macmillan Company, 1931.

Northrop, F. S. C. "The Relation between Naturalistic Scientific Knowledge and Humanistic Intrinsic Values in Western Culture," in *Contemporary American Philosophy*. Ed. J. E. Smith, 1970. London: George Allen & Unwin, 1970. pp. 107–151.

Ortega y Gasset, Jose. *Concord and Liberty*. Trans. Helen Weyl. New York: W. W. Norton and Company, Inc., 1946.

Owen, G. E. L. *Times Literary Supplement,* May 27, 1977, p. 646.

Parsons, James Bayard. "Elements, Chemical." *Encyclopaedia Britannica,* vol. 8. Expo 70 ed. Chicago: Encyclopaedia Britannica, Inc., 1970, pp. 270–273.

Plato. *The Dialogues of Plato,* 2 vols. Trans. B. Jowett. New York: Random House, 1937 (1892).

Plato. See Cornford.

Popper, K. R. *The Open Society and its Enemies,* 2 vols. Princeton: Princeton University Press, 1963.

Radhakrishnan, S. and Moore, C. A. *A Source Book in Indian Philosophy*. Princeton, New Jersey: Princeton University Press, 1957.

Rasmussen, Steen Eilen. *Experiencing Architecture*. Cambridge, MA: M.I.T. Press, 1962.

Rist, J. M. *Stoic Philosophy*. Cambridge: The University Press, 1969.

Rostovtsev, Mikhail Ivanovich. *Rome*. Trans. J. D. Duff. Galaxy book ed.

prepared with the assistance of Elias J. Bickerman. New York: Oxford University Press, 1960.

Rostovtsev, Mikhail Ivanovich. *Greece*. Trans. J. D. Duff. New York: Oxford University Press, 1963.

Russell, Bertrand. *The Wisdom of the West*. Ed. Paul Foulkes. London: Macdonald and Company, Ltd., 1959.

Sandbach, F. H. *The Stoics*. New York: W. W. Norton & Company, 1975.

Scott, Samuel P. *The Civil Law,* 17 vols., *The Digest,* vol. 3. Cincinnati: The Central Trust Company, 1932.

Smith, Allen E. and Diane M. Secoy. "Forerunners of Pesticides in Classical Greece and Rome." *Journal of Agricultural Food Chemistry* (Nov.–Dec. 1975):1050–55.

Sohm, Rudolph. *The Institutes,* 3rd ed. New York: Augusta M. Kelley, 1970 (1940).

Sohm, Rudolph. *Institutes of Roman Law*. Trans. James C. Ledlie. (3rd English ed. based on 12th German ed.) Cambridge: Clarendon Press, 1907.

St. Louis Post-Dispatch 98:159. "New Subatomic Particle Discovered." (June 9, 1976): 1A.

Teilhard de Chardin, Pierre. *The Phenomenon of Man*. New York: Harper & Row, 1965.

Thayer, Horace Standish, ed. *Newton's Philosophy of Nature: Selections From His Writings*. New York: Hafner, 1953, 1960.

Vlastos, Gregory. *Plato's Universe*. Seattle: University of Washington Press, 1975.

Westrup, Carl W. *Introduction to Early Roman Law,* 4 volumes. London: Oxford University Press, 1944.

Whitehead, Alfred North, "Mathematics as an Element in the History of Thought," in *The World of Mathematics,* 4 vols. Ed., Newman. New York: Simon and Schuster, 1956. pp. 402–416.

Wolff, Hans Julius. "Greek Law." *Encyclopaedia Britannica,* vol. 8, 15th ed. Chicago: Encyclopaedia Britannica, Inc., 1975. pp. 398–402.

Wolff, Hans Julius. "Greek Legal History–Its Functions and Potentialities." *Washington University Law Quarterly* 395 (1975).

Young, Thomas Frazer. "Air." *Encyclopaedia Britannica,* vol. 1. Expo 70 ed. Chicago: Encyclopaedia Britannica, Inc., 1970. pp. 418–419.

Index